STARTER
WORKBOOK
with Digital Pack

CEFR
A1

TH!NK
SECOND EDITION

Herbert Puchta,
Jeff Stranks &
Peter Lewis-Jones

with Vicki Anderson

CAMBRIDGE
UNIVERSITY PRESS

ACKNOWLEDGEMENTS

Author

The authors and publishers acknowledge the following sources of copyright material and are grateful for the permissions granted. While every effort has been made, it has not always been possible to identify the sources of all the material used, or to trace all copyright holders. If any omissions are brought to our notice, we will be happy to include the appropriate acknowledgements on reprinting and in the next update to the digital edition, as applicable.

Key: UW = Unit Welcome; U = Unit.

Photography

All the photographs are sourced from Getty Images.

UW: Westend61; David Crespo/Moment; Vostok/Moment; Elen11/iStock/Getty Images Plus; Prasit photo/Moment; Barcin/iStock/Getty Images Plus; WIN-Initiative/Stone; Vesnaandjic/E+; Tharakorn Arunothai/EyeEm; Vesna Jovanovic/EyeEm; Mint Images/Mint Images RF; Barry Wong/The Image Bank; Rainer Grosskopf/Photolibrary; Ng Sok Lian/EyeEm; hudiemm/E+; monkeybusinessimages/iStock/Getty Images Plus; Circle Creative Studio/iStock/Getty Images Plus; MmeEmil/E+; Siri Stafford/Photodisc; **U1:** Jonathan Kirn/The Image Bank; avdeev007/E+; filipefrazao/iStock/Getty Images Plus; LeoPatrizi/E+; Rifka Hayati/E+; Mike Kemp; AfricaImages/iStock/Getty Images Plus; Henrik5000/E+; prill/iStock/Getty Images Plus; Quality Sport Images/Getty Images Sport; Kelly Defina/Getty Images Sport; Sorapong Chaipanya/EyeEm; 10'000 Hours/DigitalVision; shaunl/iStock/Getty Images Plus; Thurtell/E+; Poligrafistka/DigitalVision Vectors; fstop123/E+; Kypros/Moment; Morsa Images/DigitalVision; FLMfotografia/Fernando Lobos Miralles/Moment Open; Compassionate Eye Foundation/DigitalVision; mtreasure/iStock/Getty Images Plus; Marcel Germain/Moment; luoman/E+; Yoshio Tomii/Photolibrary; **U2:** monkeybusinessimages/iStock/Getty Images Plus; FatCamera/E+; Westend61; Aditya Sethia/EyeEm; **U3:** Danielle Kiemel/Moment; MargaretW/iStock/Getty Images Plus; gerenme/iStock/Getty Images Plus; petrenkod/iStock/Getty Images Plus; Jason Finn/iStock/Getty Images Plus; LeeYiuTung/iStock/Getty Images Plus; medusaphotography/iStock/Getty Images Plus; anmbph/iStock/Getty Images Plus; RuthBlack/iStock/Getty Images Plus; Thomas Barwick/Stone; svetikd/E+; Hazmi Che Man/EyeEm; Obradovic/E+; John Slater/The Image Bank Unreleased; **U4:** Maskot; Image Source; Feifei Cui-Paoluzzo/Moment; Rafael Ben-Ari/The Image Bank; mindscanner/iStock/Getty Images Plus; violinconcertono3/iStock/Getty Images Plus; AlixKreil/iStock/Getty Images Plus; Violetta Potapova/EyeEm; Guerilla; Yellow Dog Productions/DigitalVision; akinshin/iStock/Getty Images Plus; fcafotodigital/E+; sanchesnet1/iStock/Getty Images Plus; scanrail/iStock/Getty Images Plus; Yevgen Romanenko/Moment; **U5:** Sol de Zuasnabar Brebbia/Moment; Thomas Barwick/Stone; **U6:** wagnerokasaki/E+; Indeed; Paul Vozdic/The Image Bank; Rick Gomez; SerhiiBobyk/iStock/Getty Images Plus; Westend61; Fuse/Corbis; Mint Images/Mint Images RF; triocean/iStock/Getty Images Plus; SolStock/E+; kate_sept2004/E+; Paul Bradbury/OJO Images; shapecharge/E+; Artem Varnitsin/EyeEm; Lane Oatey/Blue Jean Images; skynesher/E+; Wavebreakmedia/iStock/Getty Images Plus; **U7:** gazanfer/iStock/Getty Images Plus; JoyImage/iStock/Getty Images Plus; Bryn Lennon/Getty Images Sport; Junya Nishigawa - PARAPHOTO/Getty Images Sport; Fuse/Corbis; kyoshino/iStock/Getty Images Plus; **U8:** Inti St Clair; joingate/iStock/Getty Images Plus; Kim Grosz/EyeEm; **U9:** Emma Farrer/Moment; Science Photo Library; Floortje/E+; Byjeng/iStock/Getty Images Plus; Yothin Sanchai/EyeEm; Natthakan Jommanee/EyeEm; Nattawut Lakjit/EyeEm; bergamont/iStock/Getty Images Plus; eli_asenova/E+; ManuWe/E+; Creativeye99/E+; FotografiaBasica/iStock/Getty Images Plus; Getty Images/EyeEm; Marat Musabirov/iStock/Getty Images Plus; Hyrma/iStock/Getty Images Plus; Nirut Punshiri/EyeEm; LauriPatterson/E+; pamela_d_mcadams/iStock/Getty Images Plus; Simon Belcher; AnnaPustynnikova/iStock/Getty Images Plus; Nettiya Nithascharukul/EyeEm; Burcu Atalay Tankut/Moment; **U10:** Underwood Archives/Archive Photos; WPA Pool/Getty Images News; IMAGEMORE Co.,Ltd.; Sylvain Lefevre/Getty Images Entertainment; Print Collector/Hulton Archive; George Pachantouris/Moment; Jesse Grant/Getty Images Entertainment; Noam Galai/Getty Images Entertainment; Topical Press Agency/Hulton Archive; INDRANIL MUKHERJEE/AFP; UniversalImagesGroup/Universal Images Group; Universal History Archive/Universal Images Group; SDI Productions/E+; **U11:** izusek/E+; moodboard; MichaelJust/iStock/Getty Images Plus; Chris McNeill/500px Prime; Fernán Quetequitenloviajao/500Px Plus; by Simon Gakhar/Moment Open; CreativeNature_nl/iStock/Getty Images Plus; Mark Hamblin/Oxford Scientific; Andrea Edwards/EyeEm; Philartphace/E+; shuchun ke/500px/500Px Plus; Maria Jeffs/iStock/Getty Images Plus; Sergio Amiti/Moment; kickers/E+; Image Source; DEA PICTURE LIBRARY/De Agostini Picture Library; FierceAbin/E+; Richard Nowitz/DigitalVision; **U12:** Mike Kemp; Luis Franceschi/EyeEm; Steve Raymer/Corbis D;ocumentary; wsfurlan/E+; MicroStockHub/iStock/Getty Images Plus; simonbradfield/E+.

The following photographs are sourced from other sources/libraries.

U2: Courtesy of LBI Entertainment, LLC; **U10:** Mike Blenkinsop/Alamy Stock Photo.

Cover photography by Konstantin Tronin/Shutterstock; © Marco Bottigelli/Moment/Getty Images

Illustrations

UW: Ben Scruton; Adam Linley; Emma Nyari; **U1**: Ben Scruton; Martin Sanders; Mark Ruffle; **U2**: Dusan Lakicevic; emc design ltd; **U3**: Ben Scruton; Adam Linley; Mark Ruffle; Martin Sanders; **U4**: Martin Sanders; Adam Linley; Martin Sanders; Dusan Lakicevic; Mark Ruffle; **U5**: Dusan Lakicevic; Adam Linley; Mark Ruffle; **U6**: Emma Nyari; Ben Scruton; **U7**: Dusan Lakicevic; Ben Scruton; Adam Linley; Mark Ruffle; **U8**: Emma Nyari; **U9** & **U10**: Adam Linley; **U11**: Mark Ruffle; **U12**: Dusan Lakicevic; Martin Sanders; Adam Linley.

The Vlog & Grammar Rap Video Stills: Silversun Media Group

Audio Production: Leon Chambers

CONTENTS

WELCOME

The alphabet

1 🔊 W.01 **Listen and write the names and the cities.**

Names

0 _B o b b y_
1 _ _ _ _ _
2 _ _ _ _ _ _ _
3 _ _ _ _ _
4 _ _ _ _ _ _ _ _
5 _ _ _ _ _

Cities

6 _ _ _ _ _
7 _ _ _ _ _ _
8 _ _ _ _ _ _ _ _
9 _ _ _ _ _ _ _
10 _ _ _ _ _
11 _ _ _ _ _ _

2 **Match to make the words.**

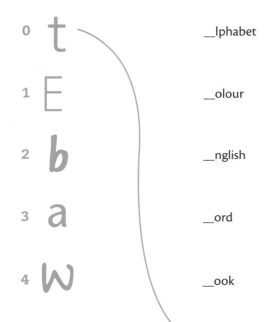

0 t   __lphabet

1 E   __olour

2 b   __nglish

3 a   __ord

4 w   __ook

5 c   _t_ hink

Colours

3 🔊 W.02 **Listen and write the colours. Then colour the pictures in the correct colour.**

0 _b l a c k_   1 _ _ _ _   2 _ _ _ _ _ _

3 _ _ _ _ _ _   4 _ _ _ _ _   5 _ _ _ _ _

6 _ _ _ _ _ _ _   7 _ _ _ _ _ _ _   8 _ _ _ _ _

9 _ _ _ _ _ _ _   10 _ _ _ _ _

4 **Find ten more colours in the word search and colour the squares in the correct colour.**

b	l	a	c	k	u	y	d	e	r
e	g	r	e	e	n	e	e	e	b
n	o	y	d	w	x	l	g	u	a
w	w	e	o	k	l	n	l	c
o	h	r	r	k	n	o	a	b	k
r	i	g	n	e	i	w	r	e	y
b	t	i	g	k	p	u	o	l	i
p	e	p	e	l	p	r	u	p	g

International words

5 **Put the letters in order to make words.**

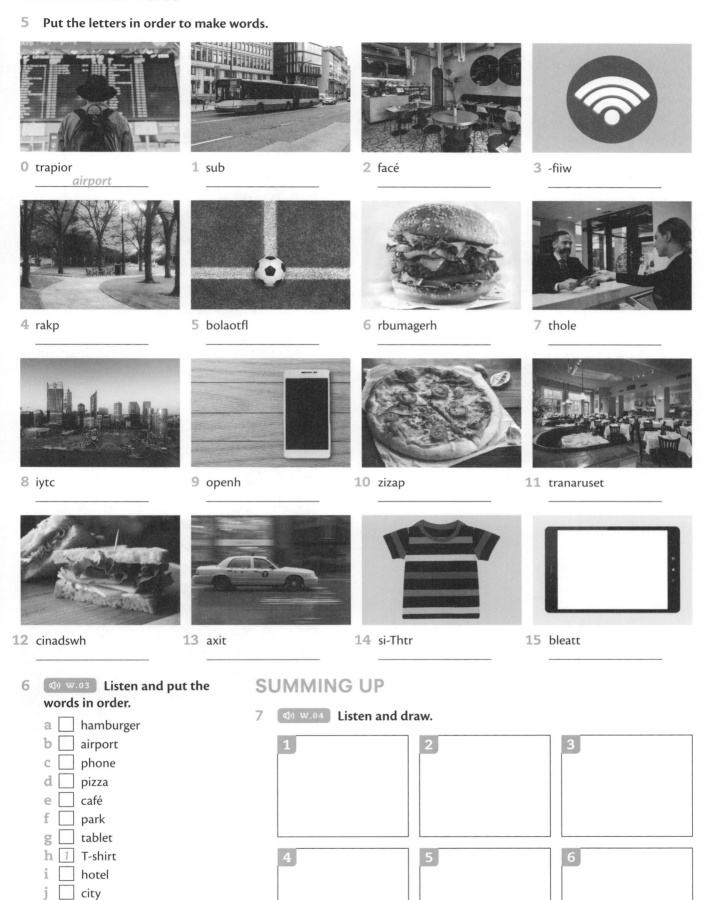

0 trapior
airport

1 sub
_____

2 facé
_____

3 -fiiw
_____

4 rakp
_____

5 bolaotfl
_____

6 rbumagerh
_____

7 thole
_____

8 iytc
_____

9 openh
_____

10 zizap
_____

11 tranaruset
_____

12 cinadswh
_____

13 axit
_____

14 si-Thtr
_____

15 bleatt
_____

6 🔊 W.03 **Listen and put the words in order.**

a ☐ hamburger
b ☐ airport
c ☐ phone
d ☐ pizza
e ☐ café
f ☐ park
g ☐ tablet
h ☐ 1 T-shirt
i ☐ hotel
j ☐ city

SUMMING UP

7 🔊 W.04 **Listen and draw.**

1	2	3
4	5	6

Articles: *a* and *an*

1   ⟨Circle⟩ the correct options.

0   *a* / *an* orange bus
1   *a* / *an* grey airport
2   *a* / *an* American TV
3   *a* / *an* white tablet
4   *a* / *an* English actor
5   *a* / *an* hamburger
6   *a* / *an* black taxi
7   *a* / *an* phone
8   *a* / *an* Italian car
9   *a* / *an* red bus

2   **Write the words in the list in the correct columns. Then write five more words in each column.**

> actor | airport | apple | ~~city~~
> hamburger | hotel | orange | taxi

a	*an*
city	

The day

3   **Look at the pictures and complete the phrases.**

0   Good
    m o r n i n g

2   Good
    _ _ _ _ _ _

1   Good
    _ _ _ _ _ _ _ _

3   Good
    _ _ _ _ _ _ _ _ _ _

Saying *Hello* and *Goodbye*

4   **Write the words in the list under the pictures.**

> Bye | Good afternoon
> Good evening | Good morning
> Good night | ~~Hello~~ | Hi | See you

A

    Hello.   _____

_____   _____

B

_____   _____

_____   _____

SUMMING UP

5 **W.05** **Put the conversations in order. Then listen and check.**

Conversation 1

☐ **Holly** Good morning, Mr Wood.
☐ **Holly** I'm fine. And you?
☐ **Mr Wood** Hello, Holly. How are you?
☐ **Mr Wood** I'm great, thanks.

Conversation 2

☐ **Nick** Yeah, have a good day.
☐ **Nick** Bye, Jodie.
☐ **Jodie** Bye, Nick. See you later.

Conversation 3

☐ **Alex** I'm fine, thank you.
☐ **Alex** Bye, Mrs Young.
☐ **Alex** Good afternoon, Mrs Young.
☐ **Mrs Young** Good. I'll see you in class.
☐ **Mrs Young** Hello, Alex. How are you?

6 **Write short dialogues.**

Carmen _____ *Hello.* _____
Leo _____
Jake _____
Carmen _____

Dora _____
Dad _____

Classroom objects

1 **Match the pictures with the words in the list. Write 1–10 in the boxes.**

> **1** book | **2** chair | **3** computer
> **4** ~~desk~~ | **5** door | **6** pen | **7** pencil
> **8** projector | **9** board | **10** window

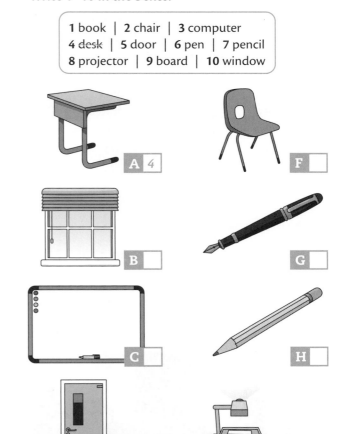

A 4
F
B
G
C
H
D
I
E
J

2 **Use the letters from Exercise 1 to complete the crossword.**

E
B   F
G
H↓ I→
C→ J↓   A
B
o
D   o
k

Numbers 0–20

3 **Write the numbers.**

0	four	_4_	11	seven	_____
1	eight	_____	12	sixteen	_____
2	twenty	_____	13	eighteen	_____
3	five	_____	14	ten	_____
4	twelve	_____	15	fourteen	_____
5	six	_____	16	three	_____
6	eleven	_____	17	thirteen	_____
7	one	_____	18	seventeen	_____
8	fifteen	_____	19	two	_____
9	nineteen	_____	20	nine	_____
10	zero	_____			

Plural nouns

4 **How many do you see? Look, count and write the plurals.**

> book | chair | child | computer | door | ~~man~~
> pencil | pen | phone | window | woman

0	eight	_men_
1	three	_____
2	seven	_____
3	fifteen	_____
4	eighteen	_____
5	two	_____
6	one	_____
7	zero	_____
8	twelve	_____
9	four	_____
10	six	_____

Classroom language

5 **Circle the correct options.**

0 Close your books. /
(What does this mean?)

4 Listen. /
Look at the picture.

1 Put up your hand. /
Close your books.

5 Work with a partner. /
Put up your hand.

2 Listen. / That's right.

6 Open your books. /
Look at the picture.

3 Work with a partner. /
That's wrong.

SUMMING UP

6 🔊 W.06 **Listen and tick (✓) the sentences that you hear.**

1 There are three books. ☐
2 Open your books. ☐
3 There are 20 children in the class. ☐
4 What does this mean? ☐
5 There are two windows. ☐
6 Put up your hand. ☐

Numbers 20–100

1 Write the numbers.

0 seventy   _70_
1 thirty   _____
2 forty   _____
3 ninety   _____
4 a hundred   _____
5 fifty   _____
6 twenty   _____
7 sixty   _____
8 eighty   _____
9 thirty-four   _____
10 sixty-eight   _____
11 twenty-one   _____
12 ninety-nine   _____
13 fifty-three   _____

2 ◁)) W.07 Listen and write the numbers.

0 _thirty-four_
a _____
b _____
c _____
d _____
e _____
f _____
g _____
h _____
i _____
j _____
k _____

Messages

3 ◁)) W.08 Listen to the messages and (circle) the correct options.

Message 1

Message for Joe from David [0] Jones / (James.)

His office is at number [1] 6 / 7,

[2] Thames / Temms Road.

The train station is [3] Cue / Kew Bridge.

His phone number is [4] 0207328759 /
0208686758.

Message 2

Debbie's message from Claire Greene.

The party is at the [5] Britannia / Breton Hotel.

The address of the hotel is [6] 44 / 34,
South Street.

The bus number is [7] 15 / 16.

Her phone number is 01244 [8] 5564456 /
5634453.

SUMMING UP

4 ◁)) W.09 Listen and complete the messages.

Message 1

Hi Daniel,

Message from Mr [0] _Cleverly_.

His address is [1] _____,
King Street.

The bus to get is number [2] _____.

His phone number is [3] _____
676 745.

Message 2

Hi Erica,

Message from Jane [4] _____.

Her house number is [5] _____
on Linton Road.

The name of the station is [6] _____
City.

Her phone number is 07837 [7] _____.

1 ALL TOGETHER

Grammar rap!

GRAMMAR
Question words

→ SB p.14

1 ★☆☆ **Complete the sentences with the correct question words.**

0 ___What___ is your name?
1 _____ old are you?
2 _____ are you from?
3 _____ is your favourite athlete?
4 _____ is he / she your favourite athlete?

2 ★★★ **Write answers to the questions in Exercise 1 so they are true for you.**

0 _My name is ..._
1 _____
2 _____
3 _____
4 _____

PRONUNCIATION
/h/ or /w/ in question words
Go to page 118. 🎧

3 ★★☆ **Look at the pictures and circle the correct words.**

0 *He / She / It* is happy.

1 *We / You / I* are friends.

2 *They / We / You* are Brazilian.

3 *She / He / It* is eleven.

4 *I / She / We* am Sonia.

5 *We / They / You* are Mario.

6 *We / I / They* are sisters.

7 *I / It / You* is the Turkish flag.

to be

→ SB p.15

4 ⭐☆☆ **Complete the table with the words in the list.**

| am | are | are | are | is | is | is |

0	I	*am*	Jon.
1	You		thirteen.
2	He		happy.
3	She		from Spain.
4	It		Indonesian.
5	We		sisters.
6	They		friends.

5 ⭐⭐☆ **Complete the sentences with the correct form of the verb *to be*. Use contracted forms.**

0 You*'re* Spanish.

1 I__ Mexican.

2 We__ Russian.

3 They__ Indonesian.

4 He__ American.

5 She__ Brazilian.

6 ⭐⭐☆ **Rewrite the sentences using contracted forms.**

0 It is a Japanese flag.
   It's a Japanese flag

1 She is Sudanese.
   _____

2 You are a good friend.
   _____

3 They are British.
   _____

4 We are from New York.
   _____

5 I am Andres. What is your name?
   _____

6 He is 12 today.
   _____

GET IT RIGHT!

Subject–verb agreement with *be*

We use the form of *be* that agrees with the subject.

✓ *They are from Italy.*   ✗ *They is from Italy.*

Correct the sentences.

0 There are a beautiful beach.
   There is a beautiful beach.

1 The lessons is for two hours.
   _____

2 It are cold today.
   _____

3 Are the English player good?
   _____

4 We's from Mexico.
   _____

5 My favourite country are Japan.
   _____

Az VOCABULARY
Countries and nationalities
→ SB p.14

1 ★☆☆ **Find 11 more countries in the word search. Then write the countries.**

N	H	I	S	O	C	I	X	E	M
I	B	R	A	Z	I	L	S	I	E
N	A	D	U	S	S	K	O	N	T
K	C	N	A	M	P	S	U	D	U
U	Y	E	I	F	A	L	T	O	R
E	M	Z	S	E	I	S	H	N	K
H	P	B	S	K	A	P	A	E	E
T	H	E	U	S	P	A	F	S	Y
A	C	V	R	W	K	I	R	I	J
E	J	A	P	A	N	N	I	A	Q
R	R	K	A	Y	H	B	C	N	M
E	C	U	A	D	O	R	A	L	D

0 ___Brazil___   6 _____
1 _____   7 _____
2 _____   8 _____
3 _____   9 _____
4 _____   10 _____
5 _____   11 _____

2 ★★☆ **Complete the words.**

0 Peter's from Cape Town. He's South Afric _an_ .

1 He's from Glasgow. He's Briti____ .

2 I'm from Mexico City. I'm Mexic____ .

3 Ella's from Chicago. She's Americ____ .

4 They're from Valencia. They're Span____ .

5 You're from Moscow. You're Russi____ .

6 My mum is from Rio de Janeiro.
  She's Brazili____ .

7 Our teacher is from Java. He's Indones____ .

8 Haruki is from Tokyo. He's Japan____ .

9 They're from Istanbul. They're Turk____ .

10 My dad is from Khartoum. He's Sudan____ .

11 Ana and Luz are from Quito.
  They're Ecuador____ .

Adjectives
→ SB p.17

3 ★☆☆ **Write the adjectives from the list under the pictures.**

big | cheap | clean | dirty | expensive
fast | new | old | slow | small

The car is ...

0 ___big___   2 _____   4 _____
1 _____   3 _____

The car is ...

5 _____   7 _____   9 _____
6 _____   8 _____

4 ★★☆ **Put the words in order to make sentences.**

0 book / English / My / new / is
  My English book is new.

1 red / Her / is / pen
  _____

2 is / house / old / Our
  _____

3 fast / bikes / Their / are
  _____

4 big / school / Our / is
  _____

5 My / small / bedroom / is
  _____

6 car / Her / expensive / is
  _____

REFERENCE

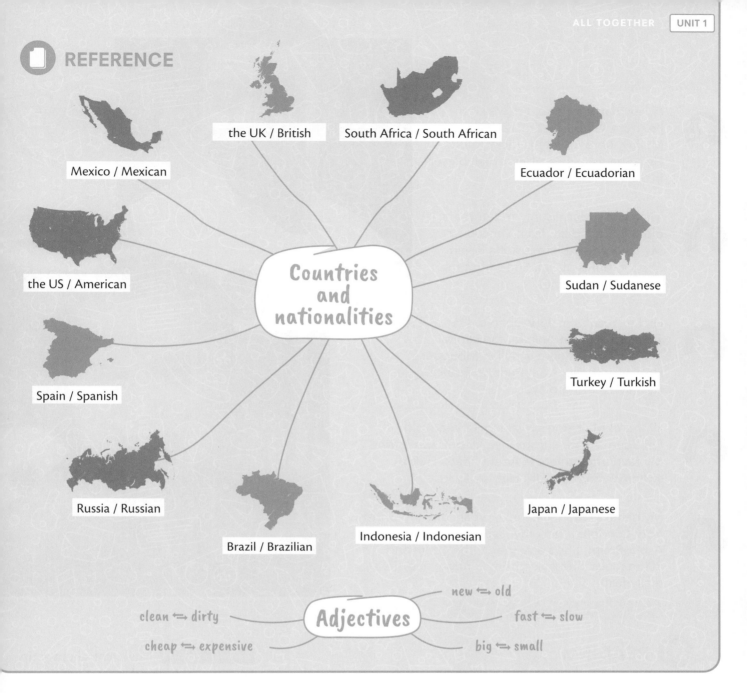

Mexico / Mexican

the UK / British

South Africa / South African

Ecuador / Ecuadorian

the US / American

Countries and nationalities

Sudan / Sudanese

Spain / Spanish

Turkey / Turkish

Russia / Russian

Brazil / Brazilian

Indonesia / Indonesian

Japan / Japanese

Adjectives

new ⇆ old

clean ⇆ dirty

fast ⇆ slow

cheap ⇆ expensive

big ⇆ small

VOCABULARY *EXTRA*

1 Write an adjective from the list under each picture.

hard | high | long | low | ~~short~~ | soft

0 ____*short*____   1 _____   2 _____   3 _____   4 _____   5 _____

2 Put the adjectives from Exercise 1 in pairs with their opposites.

_____ ⇆ _____

_____ ⇆ _____

_____ ⇆ _____

Hi, my name's Hugo. I'm Mexican. I'm from Acapulco. I'm 12 years old. My favourite athlete is Ricky Rubio. He's Spanish. He's a basketball player in the NBA. He's great.

 My name's Maddison. I'm ten years old. I'm Canadian, from Vancouver. My favourite athlete is Sofia Kenin. She's a tennis player. She's from the US. She's awesome!

 Hi, I'm Yusuf. I'm 13 years old. I'm Turkish. I'm from Ankara, the capital. My favourite athlete is Kylian Mbappé. He's a footballer from Paris, in France. He's an amazing player.

 Hi there! My name's Mia. I'm 12 years old. I'm South African, from the city of Cape Town. My favourite athlete is Adam Peaty. He's a swimmer from the UK. He's really fast.

 My name's Gabriella. I'm 11 years old. I'm British, from London. I think my favourite athlete is Dina Asher-Smith. She's a runner in the 100m and 200m races. She's also from London, and she's really fast!

READING

1 Read the texts quickly. Where are they from? Match the names with the countries.

0 Hugo   a the UK
1 Maddison   b South Africa
2 Yusuf   c Mexico
3 Mia   d Turkey
4 Gabriella   e Canada

(0 Hugo matched to c Mexico)

2 Read the texts again. Mark the sentences T (true) or F (false).

0 Hugo is from Mexico City. — F
1 Hugo's favourite athlete is a football player. ☐
2 Maddison is ten. ☐
3 Maddison's favourite athlete is a Canadian tennis player. ☐
4 Yusuf is from the capital of Turkey. ☐
5 Yusuf's favourite athlete is French. ☐
6 Mia is 11. ☐
7 Mia's favourite athlete is British. ☐
8 Gabriella's favourite athlete is a woman. ☐
9 Gabriella and Dina are from London. ☐

3 CRITICAL THINKING Now think about your favourite athlete and write.

1 What's his/her name?
_____

2 What sport does he/she do?
_____

3 Where is he/she from?
_____

4 Why is he/she your favourite athlete?
_____

About me

1 INPUT **Read the questionnaire. Where is Maria from?**

Brighton
M u s i c   A c a d e m y

Be the best – Summer Music Camp on the English Coast!
Pop, rap, reggaeton, R&B, country – we can help you be the best!

We want to know all about you.

▶ What's your name?   Maria Garcia

▶ Where are you from?   Guadalajara in Mexico

▶ How old are you?   12

▶ What's your favourite music?   pop

▶ Who's your favourite singer?   Miley Cyrus

2 ANALYSE **Complete the text about Maria with the missing words.**

> Hi, my name is ⁰____Maria____.
> I'm Mexican. I'm from ¹_____.
> I'm ²_____ years old. I love
> a lot of music! My favourite music is
> ³_____. It's great! I love rap
> and reggaeton, too. My favourite singer
> is ⁴_____. She's a singer from
> Tennessee, in the US. She's amazing!
> Her father is a country singer.

3 PLAN **Complete the questionnaire about you.**

Brighton
M u s i c   A c a d e m y

Be the Best – Summer Music Camp on the English Coast!
Pop, rap, reggaeton, R&B, country – we can help you be the best!

We want to know all about you.

▶ What's your name? _____
▶ Where are you from? _____
▶ How old are you? _____
▶ What's your favourite music? _____
▶ Who's your favourite singer? _____

4 PRODUCE **Use your answers from Exercise 3 to complete a text about you. Use the text in Exercise 2 to help you.**

> Hi, my name is _____.
> I'm _____. I'm from
> _____. I'm
> _____ old. My favourite
> music is _____. I love
> _____, too. My favourite
> _____. He's / She's
> _____. He's / She's
> _____!

✎ WRITING TIP: Checking

When you finish, always read your writing again. Check for mistakes.
• Do all the verbs agree with their subjects?

🎧 LISTENING

1 🔊 1.03 **Listen to the conversation. Number the nationalities in the order you hear them. Write 1–5 in the boxes.**

A ☐

1 _____

B ☐

2 _____

C ☐

3 _____

D ☐

4 _____

E ☐

5 _____

2 🔊 1.03 **Listen again and write the names under the photos in Exercise 1.**

> Alice | Ben | Afia | Miguel | Santi

3 **Circle the correct answers (A or B).**

0 Afia is from …
   Ⓐ Sudan   B Spain
1 Santi is from …
   A Seville   B Shanghai
2 Ben is from …
   A Chile   B Spain
3 Alice is from …
   A the UK   B Ecuador
4 Miguel is from …
   A London   B Quito

DIALOGUE

4 **Circle the correct answers (A, B or C) to complete the conversation.**

Boy Hi, what's your name?
Girl I'm 0 A 12.
                B Brazil.
                Ⓒ Alex.
Boy And where are you from?
Girl 1 A I'm Canadian.
             B I'm 11.
             C Sara.
Boy What city are you from?
Girl 2 A Japan.
             B Toronto.
             C Mexico.
Boy Toronto's a beautiful city.
Girl 3 A Yes, I am.
             B Yes, it is.
             C Yes, they are.
Boy Who's your favourite singer?
Girl 4 A Shawn Mendes.
             B Lionel Messi.
             C Yes.
Boy Why is he your favourite singer?
Girl 5 A No.
             B Yes.
             C Because he's so awesome.
Boy Nice to meet you, Alex.
Girl 6 A Yes.
             B No.
             C Nice to meet you, too.

PHRASES FOR FLUENCY → SB p.18

5 **Match the phrases (1–4) with their meanings (a–d).**

1 How's it going?   a Goodbye.
2 See you later.   b How are you?
3 I know.   c Great.
4 That is so awesome!   d You're right.

6 **Use the phrases 1–4 from Exercise 5 to complete the dialogues.**

1 A Hi, David. _____
   B I'm fine, thanks.
2 A Bye, Tomas.
   B Bye, Lina. _____
3 A This is my new tablet.
   B _____
4 A Raheem's a great football player.
   B _____

SUM IT UP

1 Where do you see these things?

1

A the US
B the UK
C Italy

3

A Mexico
B Brazil
C China

2

A the US
B Australia
C Russia

4

A Japan
B the US
C Spain

2 Where do they say 'hello' like this?

1 'How's it going?'
A the US
B Portugal
C Colombia

2 'Buenos dias'
A Argentina
B Turkey
C Australia

3 'Konnichiwa'
A Russia
B China
C Japan

4 'Merhaba'
A Russia
B Turkey
C Ecuador

3 Where are these capital cities?

1 Paris
A Sudan
B France
C Italy

2 Pretoria
A The UK
B Mexico
C South Africa

3 Ankara
A Morocco
B Turkey
C Spain

4 Brasilia
A France
B Russia
C Brazil

4 Who is from ...

1 Brazil?
A Neymar
B Kylian Mbappé
C Ed Sheeran

2 the UK?
A Taylor Swift
B Simone Biles
C Lewis Hamilton

3 Spain?
A Lady Gaga
B Ricky Rubio
C Post Malone

4 the US?
A Gigi Hadid
B Harry Kane
C Shawn Mendes

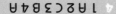

4 1A 2C 3B 4A   3 1A 2C 3B 4C   2 1A 2A 3C 4B   1 1B 2A 3B 4B

2 I'M EXCITED

Grammar rap! ▶05

ⓖ GRAMMAR

to be (negative, singular and plural) → SB p.22

1 ★☆☆ **Circle** the correct form of *to be*.

0 Joao (is) / *am* happy today. It ('s) / *'re* his birthday.

1 We *am* / *are* excited. We *'s* / *'re* on holiday.

2 It *'s* / *'m* late. I *'s* / *'m* tired.

3 Elena and Ana *is* / *are* happy. They *is* / *are* in the tennis team.

4 You *are* / *is* angry.

5 It *is* / *are* hot here.

2 ★★☆ **Complete the sentences with the correct negative form of *to be*.**

0 I ___*'m not*___ tired. I'm worried.

1 Paulo _____ happy. He's bored.

2 Zehra and Jane _____ worried. They're excited.

3 We _____ angry with you. We're worried about you, that's all.

4 Marina _____ happy at her new school. Her new classmates _____ very friendly.

5 It _____ hot in here. It's cold. Close the window.

6 I _____ hungry. I'm thirsty.

to be (questions and short answers) → SB p.23

3 ★★☆ **Circle** the correct form of *to be*.

1 A *Is* / (*Are*) Julia and Matt with you?
  B No, they *isn't* / *aren't*.

2 A *Am* / *Is* I in your team?
  B Yes, you *is* / *are*.

3 A *Am* / *Are* you on the beach now?
  B No, we *isn't* / *aren't*.

4 A *Is* / *Are* Nico at home?
  B No, he *isn't* / *aren't*.

5 A *Is* / *Are* Erin at school today?
  B Yes, she *is* / *are*.

6 A *Am* / *Are* you American?
  B No, I *'m not* / *aren't*.

4 ★★☆ **Write the questions. Then write answers so they are true for you.**

0 your name / Maria?
  Is your name Maria?   *No, it isn't.*

1 you / 15?
  _____   _____

2 you / British?
  _____   _____

3 your mum / a teacher?
  _____   _____

4 your dad / from Scotland?
  _____   _____

5 you / happy?
  _____   _____

6 your / classmates / friendly?
  _____   _____

5 ★★☆ **Complete the text messages with the correct form of *to be*.**

Hi Evie. 0 ___*Are*___ you happy? 1_____ your new school OK? 2_____ the students friendly? 3_____ it sunny there? It 4_____ sunny here. School 5_____ the same without you. Text me.

Hi Layla. I 6_____ happy. School 7_____ very different here in Australia. There 8_____ ten boys and 12 girls in my class. The girls 9_____ very friendly but the boys 10_____ . It 11_____ very hot and sunny here. And guess what? There 12_____ a swimming pool in the playground. It 13_____ all bad!

Object pronouns

→ SB p.25

6 ★☆☆ **Complete the sentences with *me*, *him*, *her*, *us*, *you* and *them*.**

My new school

0 My new school is excellent. I really like _____*it*_____ .

1 The school lunches are great. I like _____ .

2 Our English teacher is Mrs Davis. I like _____ .

3 We are good students. Mrs Davis is very happy with _____ .

4 Tim is my best friend here. He's great. I really like _____

5 Are you friendly? Do your classmates like _____ ?

6 I'm friendly. My classmates like _____ .

7 ★★☆ **Complete the dialogues so they are true for you. Use object pronouns.**

0 **A** Do you like ___*Frenkie de Jong*___ ? (name of a sports person)

   B Yes, I really like ____*him*____ .

1 **A** Do you like _____ ? (name of a female singer)

   B Yes, I like _____ . She's great.

2 **A** Do you like _____ ? (name of pop group)

   B No, I don't like _____ . They're terrible.

3 **A** Do you like _____ ? (name of a male actor)

   B Yes, I like _____ . He's an excellent actor.

4 **A** Do you like _____ ? (name of a comedy film)

   B Yes, I like _____ . It's very funny.

8 ★★★ **Write questions with *like* and the word in brackets. Then write answers so they are true for you.**

0 Demi Lovato? (you)

   Do you like Demi Lovato?

   Yes, I like her. She's a great singer.

1 the TV programme *Stranger Things*? (you)

   _____

   _____

2 football? (your dad)

   _____

   _____

3 Imagine Dragons? (your best friend)

   _____

   _____

4 Cardi B? (you)

   _____

   _____

5 comedy films? (your mum)

   _____

   _____

6 the song *Dance Monkey* by Tones and I? (you)

   _____

   _____

7 pop music? (your parents)

   _____

   _____

GET IT RIGHT!

Object pronouns

We use *it* in the singular and *them* in the plural.

✓ *I don't want this sweet. You have it.*

✓ *I don't want these sweets. You have them.*

✗ *I don't want these sweets. You have it.*

(Circle) **the correct options.**

0 This is my school. I like (it) / *them*.

1 I play computer games. I like *it* / *them*.

2 My dad has a really cool phone. I want *it* / *them*!

3 My country is small but I like *it* / *them* a lot.

4 Maroon 5? I don't like *it* / *them*.

5 My friends are here. I play football with *it* / *them* every afternoon.

6 Here is my homework. I finished *it* / *them* this morning.

VOCABULARY
Adjectives to describe feelings

→ SB p.22

1 ★☆☆ **Put the letters in order to make adjectives.**

0 r e d i t _____tired_____
1 x c e t i e d _____
2 o r r w i e d _____
3 y a n g r _____
4 o r b e d _____
5 o h t _____
6 s t y i r t h _____
7 d a s _____
8 d l o c _____
9 g r y n u h _____

2 ★★☆ **Complete the sentences with the adjectives from Exercise 1.**

0 It's late and you're ____tired____ . Go to bed.
1 My new bike is broken. My dad's _____ with me.
2 I'm _____ . Let's play a game on your tablet.
3 My friends are _____ . There's a basketball match at our school today.
4 There's an exam at school today. Amy's _____ .
5 Pedro's dog is ill. He's _____ .
6 I'm hot and _____ . Can I have a drink?
7 He's _____ . He wants a sandwich.
8 It's winter. It's _____ .
9 We're _____ . Let's go for a swim!

3 ★★★ **Circle the correct adjectives.**

0 A Are you (worried) / excited about the exam tomorrow?
   B No, I'm not. It's an easy exam.
1 A Is Azra excited / bored about the holiday?
   B Yes, she is.
2 A It's cold / hot today. Let's have an ice cream.
   B Yes, OK. That's a good idea.
3 A Are you hungry / thirsty?
   B Yes, I am.
   A Let's have some spaghetti, then.
4 A It's really hot / cold in here.
   B You're right. Let's close the window.
5 A I'm really tired / thirsty.
   B Here's a bottle of water.
   A Thanks.
6 A Mum's angry / sad with you.
   B Why?
   A You're home late.

Positive and negative adjectives
→ SB p.25

4 ★★☆ **Put the letters in order to make adjectives.**

0 He's a ____bad____ actor. (dba)
1 She's a _____ player. (ogod)
2 São Paulo is a _____ city. (arget)
3 The weather today _____ . (fluwa)
4 It's a _____ TV programme. (unfyn)
5 There's an exam today. It's _____ ! (ritlerbe)
6 The sandwiches here are _____ . (etnlcxele)
7 Volleyball is an _____ sport. (igecntix)

5 ★☆☆ **Complete the sentences so they are true for you.**

0 ___Ariana Grande___ is a great singer.
1 _____ is a good book.
2 _____ is a funny actor/actress.
3 _____ is a terrible sport.
4 _____ is a great tennis player.
5 _____ is an exciting city.
6 _____ is an awful computer game.
7 _____ is a bad song.
8 _____ and _____ are excellent games.

6 ★★☆ **Complete the dialogues so they are true for you. Use Yes, I do or No, I don't and an adjective from the list.**

awful | bad | excellent | exciting
funny | good | great | terrible

0 A Do you like football?
   B ___Yes, I do___ . It's a(n) ___great___ sport.
1 A Do you like swimming?
   B _____ . It's a(n) _____ sport.
2 A Do you like the Harry Potter books?
   B _____ . They're _____ books.
3 A Do you like basketball?
   B _____ . It's a(n) _____ game.
4 A Do you like Paul Pogba?
   B _____ . He's a(n) _____ football player.
5 A Do you like the Spider-Man films?
   B _____ . They're _____ films.

PRONUNCIATION
Vowel sounds – adjectives **Go to page 118.** 🎧

REFERENCE

ADJECTIVES TO DESCRIBE FEELINGS

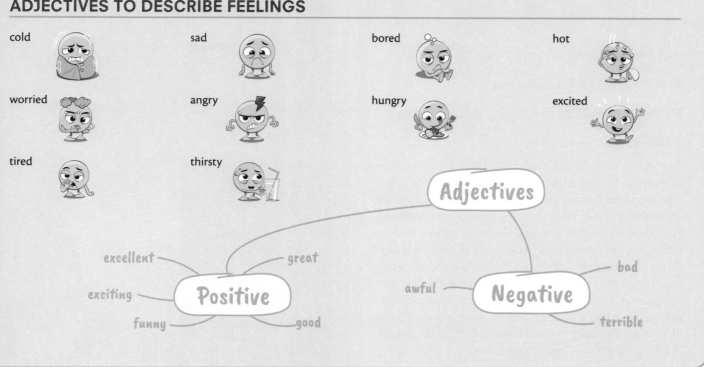

cold

sad

bored

hot

worried

angry

hungry

excited

tired

thirsty

Adjectives

excellent   great

exciting   Positive

funny   good

awful   Negative   bad

terrible

VOCABULARY *EXTRA*

1   **Match the pictures with an adjective from the list.**

afraid | difficult | easy | happy | heavy | strong

0   _afraid_

1 _____

2 _____

3 _____

4 _____

5 _____

2   **Complete the sentences with the correct adjective from Exercise 1.**

1   A lot of people find maths _____ .

2   Milou is _____ today – it's her birthday.

3   Some children are _____ of the dark at night.

4   My mum's suitcase is _____ – it's 23 kg!

5   Rugby players are very _____ .

6   It's _____ to make a cup of tea.

A young star

NAME: Grace Avery VanderWaal

NATIONALITY: American

PLACE OF BIRTH: Lenaxa, Kansas, the US

LIKES: films, music, books

The year is 2020. Grace VanderWaal is at school in Suffern, in New York. She's 15 and she's excited. She loves high school and her friends there. Grace is a winner of the TV show *America's Got Talent*. Her parents are not musicians. Her mother's name is Tina and her father's name is David. Grace has a brother called Jakob, and a sister called Olivia. Grace is a pop singer. She plays the ukulele and writes her own songs. She's also an actress in a Disney film called *Stargirl*. Her YouTube channel is famous and she plays with groups like Imagine Dragons and Florence and the Machine. Her music is popular in the US, Europe, Australia and Japan. Maybe it's popular in your country, too!

WHO ARE HER MUSICAL HEROES?

Jason Mraz and Katy Perry

DOES SHE LIKE SOCIAL MEDIA?

Yes, she does. She's on Facebook and Instagram, and has millions of followers.

WHAT DOES SHE LIKE?

Grace likes films (her favourite is *Breakfast at Tiffany's*), reading, writing songs and school!

READING

1 **Read the profile of a young singer. Find and <u>underline</u> the answers to these questions.**

   1 Why is she famous?
   2 Which film is she in?

2 **Read the profile again and write short answers to the questions.**

   0 Is her nationality British?   *No, it isn't.*
   1 Is Grace happy at school?   _____
   2 Is Grace from New York?   _____
   3 Are her parents musicians?   _____
   4 Is she an actress?   _____
   5 Does she like Jason Mraz?   _____
   6 Does she like films?   _____
   7 Are songs important to her?   _____
   8 Is she popular in your country? _____

3 CRITICAL THINKING **Read the text again. Mark the sentences T (true) or F (false) for Grace.**

   1 I think high school is great.   ☐
   2 All my family are good musicians.   ☐
   3 I am only good at singing.   ☐
   4 The old films are the best!   ☐

DEVELOPING *Writing*

A text message

1 INPUT **Read the text messages and write P (positive) or N (negative) below each message.**

a Hi, Diana. Are you still bored? Read a book! My favourite book is *Little Women*. It's a great story. I really like Jo. She's friendly and funny. Sometimes it's sad 😞 , but the ending is happy 😊! Please read it.

Naomi ☐

b Hi, Mark. I'm at the cinema. The film is terrible. I don't like it. The actors are very bad. I don't like them. I'm really bored. Where are you? Text me.

Toni ☐

c Hi, Josh. Are you at home? Listen to this song. It's great! The singer is excellent. The guitarist is good. I really like it. Do you? Tell me what you think.

Lara ☐

d Hi, Sam. Thank you for the film. It's very funny. I really like it. My sister likes it, too. Rebel Wilson is great! She's a very clever actress. The other actors are good, too. Speak soon.

Daisy ☐

e Hi, Patri. This song is terrible! How is it number one? The singer is awful and the words are boring. I really don't like it. My friends don't like it. Why is it popular? What do you think? Text me!!!

Adam ☐

2 ANALYSE **Find and write all of the adjectives from Exercise 1 in the correct columns.**

positive	negative

3 **Look at the text messages in Exercise 1. Complete the sentences with *likes* or *doesn't like* and the correct adjective.**

0 Naomi _____*likes*_____ the story. It's _____*great*_____ .

1 Toni _____ the film. It's _____ .

2 Lara _____ the song. It's _____ .

3 Daisy _____ the film. It's _____ .

4 Adam _____ the song. It's _____ .

4 **You like a book and you want to text a friend about it. Complete the text message.**

Hi, _____ . Are you still bored? Read a book! My favourite book is _____ . It's a _____ story. I really like _____ . He/She is _____ . The ending is _____ . Please read it.

5 **You don't like a film and you want to text a friend about it. Complete the text message.**

Hi, _____ . I'm at the cinema. The film is _____ . I _____ it. The actors are _____ . I _____ them. I'm really _____ . Where are you? Text me.

6 PLAN **Think about a film, a book, a band or a song and write notes about it.**

Title: _____
like / don't like   great / terrible
_____
_____
_____

✏️ **WRITING TIP: Some useful language**

- I *like / don't like* the film.
- I *really like / love* the song.
- The *film / book / band / song* is *funny / exciting / sad.*
- The *actor(s) / singer(s)* is / are *great / terrible / awful.*
- The ending is *happy / sad.*

7 PRODUCE **Now write a short text message about the film, book, band or song. Use your notes from Exercise 6. Write 35–50 words.**

_____
_____
_____
_____

🎧 LISTENING

1 🔊 2.03 **Listen to the conversations. Which conversation (1–5) matches the photo? Write the number.**

2 🔊 2.03 **Listen again and mark the sentences T (true) or F (false).**

1 It's Emma's birthday. ☐
2 Tom is cold. ☐
3 John doesn't like English. ☐
4 Tyler doesn't like the film. ☐
5 Helen's cat is ill. ☐

3 🔊 2.03 **Listen again and circle the correct options.**

1 A Hi, Jane.
   B Oh, hi, Kate.
   A It's Emma's birthday today. Is she *happy / excited*?
   B Yes, she is. I'm *happy / excited*, too.
2 A What's the matter?
   B It's *hot / cold* in here. Are you *hot / cold*, Tom?
   A *No, I'm not. / Yes, I am.* I'm wearing a jumper.
   B Well, I'm very *hot / cold*. Can you *open / close* the window?
   A OK.
3 A There's an exam tomorrow. Are you worried, John?
   B No, I'm not worried about it. I *like / don't like* English. I'm just tired.
   A Well, I'm worried. I'm very worried. I *like / don't like* English.
4 A What's wrong, Tyler? Are you *tired / bored*?
   B No, I'm not. I'm just *tired / bored*. I don't like this film.
   A Why? I *like / don't like* it. It's very funny.
5 A What's the matter with Helen? Why is she *sad / angry*?
   B Her cat's ill. It's at the vet.
   A Oh, no. That's *sad / terrible*. Poor Helen.

DIALOGUE

4 **Complete the conversation with the words from the list.**

don't like | funny | great | ~~likes~~ | likes | terrible

A Do you like the song *Can You Feel the Love Tonight?* from the film *The Lion King*?
B No, I don't. But my little sister ⁰ _____likes_____ it. It's her favourite song. She sings it all the time. In fact, she ¹_____ all the songs from the film.
A Do you like the film?
B No, I don't. It's ²_____ . I ³_____ animation films.
A Ah, I really like it. It's a ⁴_____ film. It's ⁵_____ .

Train to TH!NK

Categorising

5 **Put the words in the list into categories. There are four words for each category.**

beach | ~~Brazil~~ | cold | New Zealand | sad
school | stadium | the US | theatre
thirsty | tired | Turkey

Countries	Feelings	Places
Brazil		

6 **Choose words that you know and put them into these three categories.**

Nationalities	Colours	Classroom things

7 **Name these three categories.**

1 _____	2 _____	3 _____
good	fourteen	Laura
great	sixty-three	Tim
terrible	one hundred	Katy

EXAM SKILLS: READING
Skimming

📖 READING TIP

- Read the questions first. Then read the text quickly.
- Think about what type of text it is. Is it an article from a newspaper? An email? A text message?
- Underline the 'important' words, such as adjectives, nouns and verbs.
- Try to answer *Wh-* questions – *Who, What, When* and *Where*.

1 Skim the text in Exercise 4. What type of text is it?

A   a newspaper article ☐
B   an email ☐
C   a text message ☐

2 Find and write these 'important' words from the text.

two adjectives to describe feelings

_____

_____

two positive adjectives

_____

_____

two negative adjectives

_____

_____

3 Complete the table with information about the text.

Who?	1 _____
What?	2 _____
When?	3 _____
Where?	4 _____

4 Read the text again and choose the correct answers (A or B).

🎧 Lucy
Samara@thinkmail.com

Hi Lucy,

I'm bored. It's my little brother Jaden's birthday today. He's eight. He's very excited. All his friends are here. It's hot and sunny. They're in the garden now. His friends from his school football team are here. So, of course, they all like football. His favourite team is Liverpool. I like Liverpool, too. They're an excellent team.

Guess what his present from me is? It's a FIFA World Cup football! Oh, and a book – *Kai and the Monkey King*. It's a great story and I really like the pictures. They're excellent.

His presents from Mum and Dad are a bike and a film. It's a really good bike, but the film is terrible. It's called *Ant-Man 2*. I don't like the Ant-man films. They aren't funny.

It's 11 o'clock – Jaden's birthday lunch is in two hours. There's a big birthday cake, too. But I'm hungry now!

See you soon,

Samara

0 Is Samara excited?

A   Yes, she is.
Ⓑ   No, she isn't.

1 Is it her brother's birthday today?

A   Yes, it is.
B   No, it isn't.

2 Is it a hot day?

A   Yes, it is.
B   No, it isn't.

3 Samara _____ Liverpool.

A   likes
B   doesn't like

4 *Kai and the Monkey King* is a/an _____ book.

A   awful
B   great

5 Samara doesn't like the *Ant-Man* films. They _____ funny.

A   are
B   aren't

6 Is Samara thirsty?

A   Yes, she is.
B   No, she isn't.

CONSOLIDATION

🎧 LISTENING

1 🔊 2.04 **Listen to Annie. Circle the correct answers (A, B or C).**

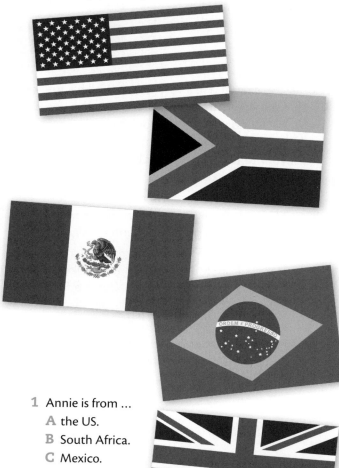

1 Annie is from …
  A the US.
  B South Africa.
  C Mexico.
2 She's …
  A 12.
  B 13.
  C 14.
3 Her best friend is from …
  A Brazil.
  B South Africa.
  C the UK.
4 Her best friend is called …
  A Paulo.
  B Pedro.
  C Marcel.

2 🔊 2.04 **Listen again. Mark the sentences T (true) or F (false).**

1 Annie is from Cape Town. ☐
2 She doesn't like sport. ☐
3 Her favourite athlete is a tennis player. ☐
4 Her favourite singer is Taylor Swift. ☐
5 Her best friend is Spanish. ☐
6 Her best friend is the same age as her. ☐

🔤 VOCABULARY

3 **Complete the sentences with words from the list. There are two extra words.**

> angry | exciting | expensive | fast | hungry | Japan
> Japanese | old | Russian | terrible | thirsty | tired

1 Singing lessons aren't cheap. They're _____ .
2 Akemi is from Japan. She's _____ .
3 Maxim is from Moscow. He's _____ .
4 The car isn't _____ . It's very slow.
5 My phone is _____ . It isn't new.
6 Dad is _____ . He isn't happy.
7 It's very late. I'm really _____ . Good night.
8 Water? Yes, please. I'm really _____ .
9 The new Avengers film is really good. It's so _____ !
10 That new restaurant is bad. The food is _____ .

Ⓖ GRAMMAR

4 **Complete the dialogues with the missing words.**

1 A Do ⁰___you___ like chocolate cake?
  B Yes, I love ¹_____ .
2 A ²_____ you like snakes?
  B No, I don't like ³_____ .
3 A Do you like Vanessa?
  B Yes, I like ⁴_____ . ⁵_____ is my best friend.
4 A Do you like Mr Henderson?
  B No, I don't like ⁶_____ . ⁷_____ 's boring.

5 **Complete the sentences with the correct form of *to be*. Use contracted forms where possible.**

0 I'm not Spanish. I ____'m____ Argentinian.
1 I _____ (✗) ten years old. I _____ 11.
2 A _____ Danny happy?
  B No, he _____ .
3 Jason and Kylie _____ from Australia.
4 A _____ you hungry?
  B Yes, we _____ .
5 Martina _____ (✗) 12. She_____ 11.
6 A Why _____ you angry?
  B Because you _____ late.
7 A How old _____ they?
  B Kevin _____ five and Gemma _____ eight.
8 A Where _____ Cathy from?
  B She _____ from South Africa.

DIALOGUE

6 **2.05 Put the conversation in order. Then listen and check.**

- ☐ **Izzy** I'm great. It's my birthday today.
- ☐ **Izzy** I know. I'm really excited.
- ☐ **Izzy** Bye.
- ☐ **Izzy** Thanks. I'm off to the new Italian restaurant.
- ☐ **Izzy** Hi, Simon, how's it going?
- ☐ **Simon** Well, have fun. See you later.
- ☐ **Simon** That is so awesome! Happy birthday!
- ☐ **Simon** Oh, hi, Izzy. I'm fine. How about you?
- ☐ **Simon** The new Italian restaurant? It's great.

READING

7 **Read the text about Rishi. Complete the information in the form.**

Personal information

Name: ⁰ _____Rishi Singh_____
Age: ¹_____
Nationality: ²_____
Likes: ³_____
Favourite athlete: ⁴_____
Favourite singer: ⁵_____
Best friend: ⁶_____

My name is Rishi Singh. I'm 13 years old. I'm from the UK. I live in Manchester. I really like sport. I like swimming and football. My favourite athlete is Kevin de Bruyne. He's a football player from Belgium. He's a midfielder and he's great. I also like music. My favourite singer is Stormzy. He's a British singer. He's really good. My best friend is Nicola. She's 13 and she's at my school.

8 **Read the text again and correct the sentences.**

0 Rishi is from the US.
Rishi is from the UK.

1 Rishi's home town is Liverpool.
_____

2 Rishi really likes rugby.
_____

3 Kevin de Bruyne is a tennis player.
_____

4 Rishi's favourite singer is a woman.
_____

5 Rishi's best friend is a boy.
_____

6 Nicola is 12.
_____

7 Nicola isn't at his school.
_____

WRITING

9 **Write a short text about you. Write 35–50 words. Use the questions to help you.**

- What is your name?
- How old are you?
- Where you are from and what is your nationality?
- What do you like?
- Who is your favourite athlete?
- Who is your favourite singer?
- Who is your best friend?

_____
_____
_____
_____
_____
_____

3 FAMILY TIME

Grammar rap!

→ 08

GRAMMAR
Possessive 's

→ SB p.32

1 ★☆☆ **Follow the lines and complete the sentences. Use 's.**

grandfather

Eva

mother

Anya

Jason

grandmother

Grayson

0 It's my _____grandfather's_____ bike.
1 It's _____ scooter.
2 It's _____ tennis racket.
3 It's my _____ book.
4 It's my _____ car.
5 It's _____ tablet.
6 It's _____ phone.

Possessive adjectives

→ SB p.33

2 ★☆☆ **Complete the table.**

	Possessive adjective
I	0 _____my_____
you	1 _____
he	2 _____
she	3 _____
we	4 _____
they	5 _____

3 ★★☆ **Joe and Nicky are at a birthday party. Circle the correct possessive adjective.**

Joe Hi! What's ¹*your / his* name?

Nicky Nicky.

Joe Is that girl ²*her / your* friend?

Nicky Well, no. That's ³*my / their* sister. ⁴*His / Her* name's Macy. This is ⁵*our / your* house.

Joe Oh. And who are those two boys?

Nicky They're ⁶*your / my* brothers. They're twins. They're 12 today. It's ⁷*their / our* birthday party. Wait a minute. Who are you?

Joe I'm Joe. I'm here with Marcus. I'm ⁸*her / his* cousin.

Nicky Oh, right.

4 ★★☆ **Complete the sentences with the correct possessive pronoun.**

0 It's George's rabbit. It's _____his_____ rabbit.
1 It's my mother's book. It's _____ book.
2 They're Jenny's sweets. They're _____ sweets.
3 It's Poppy and Sonia's tablet. It's _____ tablet.
4 It's my and my brother's TV. It's _____ TV.
5 They're Jamie's headphones. They're _____ headphones.
6 It's my grandfather's chair. It's _____ chair.
7 I have three cousins – that's _____ house.
8 That's my family's car. It's _____ car.
9 A Is that _____ phone on the table?
    B No, this is _____ phone in my hand.
10 A Is _____ friend's name Nina?
    B No, _____ name is Lena.

this / that / these / those   → SB p.34

5 ★★☆ (Circle) **the correct answers (A, B or C).**

0 _____ is my bedroom.
   (A) This   B These   C Those
1 _____ is my new games console.
   A Those   B That   C These
2 _____ are photos of my cat.
   A That   B These   C This
3 _____ computer on the table is my sister's.
   A Those   B These   C That
4 Are _____ your books over there?
   A these   B that   C those
5 Is _____ a good film?
   A these   B this   C those
6 _____ boys are from Colombia.
   A This   B That   C Those
7 _____ hotel is very expensive.
   A That   B Those   C These
8 _____ computer here is really slow.
   A That   B This   C These
9 Are _____ football players Spanish?
   A this   B these   C that
10 Is _____ his pen?
   A these   B those   C this

6 ★★☆ **Complete the sentences with *this*, *that*, *these* or *those*.**

0 ____These____ are the books I want, here.
1 _____ are my friends, over there.
2 _____ is my new phone, just here.
3 _____ are my new video games, here.
4 _____ is my father, over there.
5 _____ is my bed, right here.
6 _____ are my cousins, there.
7 _____ is my brother's laptop, right here.
8 _____ are my headphones, here.

GET IT RIGHT!

this and *these*

We use *this* to talk about singular objects that are near to us. We use *these* to talk about plural objects that are near to us.

✓ This is my favourite dress.
✗ These is my favourite dress.
✓ These are my shoes.
✗ This are my shoes.

Complete the sentences with *this* or *these*.

0 He gave me _____this_____ shirt.
1 Is _____ your pencil?
2 _____ are my favourite sweets.
3 I got _____ book yesterday.
4 Are _____ your computer games?
5 _____ are my old trainers.
6 I like _____ photo.

PRONUNCIATION
this / that / these / those Go to page 118.

VOCABULARY
Family members

→ SB p.32

1 ★☆☆ **Complete the words.**

0 au_n_t
1 _ _ o _
2 _ _ o _ _ e _
3 _ _ u _ _ a _ _
4 _ _ i _ e
5 _ _ ou _ i _
6 _ _ _ a _ _ _ _ o _ _ e _
7 _ _ _ a _ _ _ _ a _ _ e _
8 _ _ _ a _ _ _ _ o _

2 ★★☆ **Complete the sentences and the crossword with the same word. What's the mystery word?**

	1			O				
		2			T			
		3			S			
		4			H			
	5			E				
	6			E				
		7			G			

1 My _____ is 45. She's a teacher.
2 My _____ Gilly is my mother's sister.
3 My little _____ is only five years old.
4 I'm 12 and my_____ is 14.
5 My _____ is from London. He's English.
6 My _____ José is from Brazil.
7 Our teacher's _____ is a student in our class.

3 ★★★ **Write answers to the questions so they are true for you.**

1 Is your family big or small?
_____

2 What are your parents' names?
_____

3 How many cousins have you got?
_____

4 How many aunts and uncles have you got?
_____

5 Where do the people in your family live?
_____

6 How many people do you live with?
_____

House and furniture

→ SB p.35

4 ★☆☆ **Circle the odd one out in each list.**

0	bath	shower	(sofa)
1	armchair	bedroom	kitchen
2	shower	hall	dining room
3	cooker	bed	fridge
4	bedroom	toilet	living room
5	garage	kitchen	garden
6	car	hall	kitchen

5 ★★☆ **Look at the photos. Where in a house are these things? Write the words.**

0 _living room_

1 _____

2 _____

3 _____

4 _____

5 _____

6 ★★★ **Are these things in the correct place? Mark them ✓ (yes, OK) or ✗ (no).**

1 a shower in the kitchen ☐
2 a sofa in the bedroom ☐
3 a car in the garage ☐
4 a fridge in the bedroom ☐
5 a cooker in the garage ☐
6 a car in the hall ☐
7 a toilet in the bathroom ☐
8 an armchair in the garden ☐

REFERENCE
Family members

MALE	FEMALE
son	daughter
father	mother
brother	sister
grandfather	grandmother
uncle	aunt
husband	wife
grandson	granddaughter
cousin	cousin

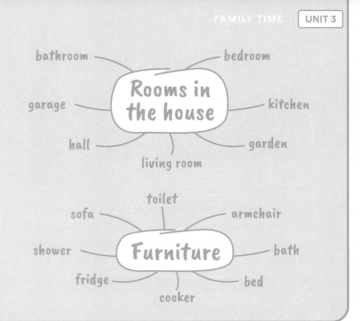

Rooms in the house: bathroom, bedroom, garage, kitchen, hall, garden, living room

Furniture: toilet, sofa, armchair, shower, bath, fridge, bed, cooker

VOCABULARY EXTRA

1 Label the drawing with the words from the list.

cup | fork | glass | knife | plate | spoon

0 _____cup_____
1 _____
2 _____
3 _____
4 _____
5 _____

2 Find the words from Exercise 1 in the word snake.

complatesuppespoonanorglasshapcupetbknifequesforkpose

PHOTO 1 _____

It's my 13th birthday today. Look! Here's my cake. I'm here at my favourite restaurant in Buenos Aires with my brothers Thiago and Nico. Thiago's my twin, so it's his birthday, too. Nico's the baby of the family. He's five.

PHOTO 2 _____

This is my grandfather's 75th birthday party. My mum and dad, three aunts, one uncle, and six cousins are all here. Aunt Claudia is my favourite aunt. She's my mother's sister. She lives in Canada with her husband Sheldon. He's Canadian. They are teachers at Toronto University. My dad's a teacher, too, and my mum's a doctor.

PHOTO 3 _____

Our house isn't big, but I have my own bedroom. It's small, but I love it! Do you like it? I have a desk for my laptop and a chair, and there's a bed, of course! I also have a wardrobe for my clothes. Thiago and Nico's bedroom is big, with two beds and Thiago's guitar.

PHOTO 4 _____

Here's Luna, my lovely rabbit, with Thiago's cat. Luna's a friendly rabbit but she's very big. The cat's name is Chester. He's very small. Luna and Chester are very good friends.

📖 READING

1 **Read the social media posts quickly. Is Emilia's family big or small?**

2 **Read the posts again and complete the sentences with words from the text.**

0 Emilia has two __brothers__ , Thiago and Nico.
1 It's Emilia and Thiago's 13th birthday. They are _____ .
2 Claudia is Emilia's favourite _____ .
3 Sheldon is from _____ .
4 Emilia's mother is a _____ .
5 Emilia's bedroom is _____ .
6 Emilia has a _____ for her clothes.
7 Her brothers have two _____ in their room.
8 Luna the rabbit is big, but she's _____ .

3 CRITICAL THINKING **Choose a title for each photo from the list and write it under the photo.**

So sweet | Love my family! | Home sweet home
I'm a teenager!

DEVELOPING Writing

My bedroom

1 INPUT **Read the text. Find five differences between Jake's perfect bedroom and his real bedroom.**

MY PERFECT BEDROOM AND MY REAL BEDROOM

My perfect bedroom is big. The walls are green and the floor is brown. The bed is very big – it's 2 metres long and 1.6 metres wide (I like big beds!). It's very comfortable, too, and it's the colour that my favourite football team plays in. So, it's black and white because my favourite team is Juventus. The desk is near the window, with a comfortable chair for me to sit, so I work on my fantastic new computer.

My real bedroom isn't big. The floor is brown, but the walls are blue. The bed is OK, but it isn't very big and it isn't very comfortable! The bed is black and white – yay! My desk is near the door and the chair is small, but it's OK. And I like my computer. It's old, but it's really good!

2 ANALYSE **Complete the sentences with *and* or *but*.**

0 The walls are red _____*and*_____ the floor is black.
1 The bed isn't very big, _____ it's comfortable.
2 The bed is comfortable _____ it's in Real Madrid colours, too.
3 The computer is old, _____ it's really good.

3 PLAN **Think about your real bedroom and about your perfect bedroom. Make notes about them.**

	My real bedroom	My perfect bedroom
big / small?		
wall colour?		
floor colour?		
big / small bed? comfortable?		
bed colour?		
near the window?		
chair? desk?		

✏ **WRITING TIP: Spelling**

When writing your description, always check that you have the correct spelling, especially for new words.

4 PRODUCE **Use your notes to write about your real bedroom. Then use your completed text and your notes to write sentences about your perfect bedroom. Write 35–50 words.**

My real bedroom
My real bedroom _____ big.
The floor is _____ and the walls are
_____ The bed is _____ .
The bed is _____ .
The _____ is near the window.
The _____ is _____ .

My perfect bedroom
_____
_____
_____
_____
_____
_____

 **LISTENING**

1 🔊 **3.03** **Listen to the conversation and complete the sentences. Write *Tony*, *Christine* or *Jack*.**

0 _____*Christine*_____ says the room is nice.

1 _____ is Tony's brother.

2 _____ likes watching football.

3 _____ loves films.

4 The games are _____'s.

2 🔊 **3.03** **Listen again and complete the words in this part of the conversation.**

Christine Wow! Are these your DVDs, Tony?
They're ⁰g___*reat*___ ! I ¹l_____ films.

Tony No, they're my brother's. He really
²l_____ old films. Very, very old films.

Christine ³W_____ a ⁴n_____ collection!

Tony Yeah. It's not bad. But the films are a
bit boring!

Christine No, they're great! Hey! Are these your games?
They're ⁵f_____ ! This one
⁶i_____ really ⁷c_____ !

Tony Yeah, I ⁸r_____ ⁹l_____ Fortnite.
It's my favourite. It's a great game.

Christine Let's play it now!

Tony OK.

DIALOGUE

3 **Put the conversations in order.**

Conversation 1

☐ **Julia** Yes, it is cool. I love T-shirts!

☐ **Julia** Happy birthday, Sienna! This is a present
for you.

☐ **Julia** This one? It's from Spain. It's a birthday
present from my Spanish friend.

☐ **Sienna** For me? Thanks, Julia! Oh, a T-shirt! And it's
really cool!

☐ **Sienna** Your T-shirt's nice, too. I really like it.

Conversation 2

☐ **Ali** Is your brother there, too?

☐ **Ali** Hi, Omer. Thanks. Wow, I really like
your house.

☐ **Omer** Thank you! Come into the living room.
My mum and dad are there.

☐ **Omer** Hi, Ali! Nice to see you. Come in!

☐ **Omer** No, he's not. He's in his bedroom.

4 **Look at Exercise 3 and complete the conversations between you and a friend.**

Conversation 1

You I really ¹*like / love* your T-shirt. Is it new?

Friend Yes, it's from ²_____ .

You It looks ³*great / nice / fantastic*.

Friend Thanks.

Conversation 2

You What ⁴*cool / great / fantastic* music!

Friend Yes, it's ⁵_____ .

You I really ⁶*like / love* it.

Friend Let's listen to more music now.

Conversation 3

You What a ⁷*fantastic / good / great* computer game!

Friend Yes. It's called ⁸_____ .

You I really ⁹*love / like* computer games.

Friend OK. Let's play it together!

5 **Now write your own conversation.**

PHRASES FOR FLUENCY → SB p.36

6 **Complete the phrases with the missing vowels.**

0 R_e_ _a_lly?

1 __h, r__ght.

2 L__t's g__ .

3 J__st _ m__n_t__ .

7 **Complete the conversation with the phrases from Exercise 6.**

Aida That boy over there is really nice.

Jon ⁰_____*Really*_____ ? Him? Well, he isn't
my favourite person.

Aida I think he looks really cool.

Jon Well, he is, but sometimes he's difficult.

Aida Hey, ¹_____ . Isn't he in your family?

Jon Yes, he's my brother.

Aida ²_____ .
Your brother. OK.

Jon Aida, ³_____ !
We're late for class!

SUM IT UP

1 **Look at the pictures and complete the crossword.**

¹B	A	²T	H

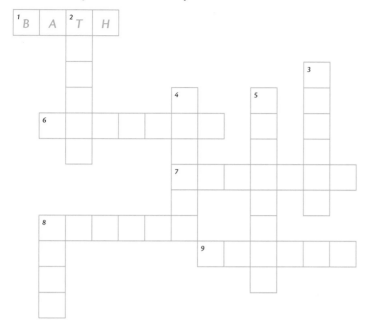

ACROSS

¹	
6	
7	
8	
9	

DOWN

2	
3	
4	
5	
8	

2 **Read a webpage about a famous house. Who lives there?**

Chatsworth House

Visit Chatsworth House! This famous house is over 450 years old. The Duke of Devonshire (he's the 12th Duke) lives here with his wife and three children, but Chatsworth House is also open for visitors. The house has over 200 rooms, 17 modern bathrooms and 459 windows. Walk round the house and imagine you are a king or a queen. See the beautiful painted hall, the state dining room, the library and bedrooms. Walk in the lovely gardens. See the farm with cows, sheep and horses!

i Open March to May and September to November, 11.00–17.00 every day. Tickets are £24.00 per adult and £14.50 for children, or £66.00 for a family of four or more.

3 **Complete the notes with information from the webpage.**

Age of house	0	*450 years old*
Family name	1	
Number of rooms	2	
Number of windows	3	
Animals on farm	4	
Opening time	5	
Closing time	6	
Months open	7	
Price per child	8	
Price for a family (4+)	9	

GRAMMAR
there is / there are

→ SB p.40

1 ★☆☆ **Complete the sentences with *is* or *are*.**

0 There _____are_____ four bedrooms in the house.

1 There _____ two Colombian girls at our school.

2 There _____ lots of famous squares in Paris.

3 There _____ a mountain near Tokyo called Mount Fuji.

4 _____ there a desk in your bedroom?

5 There _____ a small TV in my parents' bedroom.

6 There _____ nine or ten big train stations in London.

7 There _____ eight people in my family.

8 _____ there any good shops here?

2 ★★☆ **Complete the text with *there is, there isn't, there are* or *there aren't*.**

> **Julia is 14. Here is what she says about Roseland, her local shopping centre.**
>
> 'I really like our local shopping centre. It's small, but ⁰_____*there is*_____ a cinema. ¹_____ some cafés on the top floor, but ²_____ any restaurants. My mum likes it because ³_____ two good bookshops and ⁴_____ a great supermarket. My brother likes it because ⁵_____ some cool clothes shops. My dad doesn't like it because ⁶_____ a good sports shop (and he loves sport!). My sister doesn't like shopping.'

some / any

→ SB p.40

3 ★☆☆ **Circle the correct options.**

0 There are (some) / any books in my room.

1 There aren't *some* / *any* good shops here.

2 There are *some* / *any* nice curtains in their house.

3 There aren't *some* / *any* interesting books in the library.

4 There aren't *some* / *any* banks in this street.

5 There are *some* / *any* fantastic things in the museum.

6 There aren't *some* / *any* cafés in the park.

7 There are *some* / *any* supermarkets in the town centre.

8 There are *some* / *any* chairs in the garden.

4 ★★☆ **Complete the sentences with *some* or *any*.**

0 There are _____*some*_____ good shops.

1 There aren't _____ sports shops.

2 There aren't _____ cinemas.

3 There are _____ clothes shops.

4 There aren't _____ phone shops.

5 There are _____ cafés.

5 ★★☆ **Complete the text with *there is a, there isn't a, there are some* or *there aren't any*.**

> **Kerem is 12. This is what he thinks of Parkwood, his local shopping centre.**
>
> 'The shopping centre near my house is really big. There are about 200 shops in it. ⁰_____*There is a*_____ fantastic food hall. ¹_____ café with great ice creams. I like it because ²_____ good cinemas and a library, too. Mum says ³_____ good shoe shops, but they're not my favourite places. ⁴_____ games shop and ⁵_____ great clothes shops. The only bad things are that ⁶_____ electronics shops and ⁷_____ good restaurants.'

6 ★★★ Complete the questions with *Is there a / an* or *Are there any*. Then look at the texts in Exercises 2 and 5 and answer the questions. Use *Yes, there is / are*, *No, there isn't / aren't* or *I don't know*.

0 _____Is there a_____ supermarket in Roseland?
_____Yes, there is._____

1 _____ cinemas in Roseland?
_____

2 _____ electronics shop in Roseland?
_____

3 _____ clothes shops in Roseland?
_____

4 _____ sports shops in Roseland?
_____

5 _____ bank in Parkwood?
_____

6 _____ café in Parkwood?
_____

7 _____ library in Parkwood?
_____

8 _____ music shops in Parkwood?
_____

9 _____ good restaurants in Parkwood?
_____

7 ★★★ Complete these sentences so they are true for a shopping centre that you go to.

1 There are _____.
2 There aren't _____.
3 There aren't _____.
4 There are _____.
5 There is _____.
6 There isn't _____.

Imperatives

→ SB p.41

8 ★☆☆ Circle the correct options.

0 OK, everyone. Please (listen) / *don't listen* to me. This is important.
1 Are you tired? *Go / Don't go* to bed late tonight.
2 Please *be / don't be* quiet in the library.
3 It's cold in here. *Open / Don't open* the window, please.
4 Hello. Please come in and *sit / don't sit* down.
5 Wow! *Look / Don't look* at that fantastic statue.
6 It's a very expensive shop! *Buy / Don't buy* your new clothes there!
7 To get to the cinema, *turn / don't turn* left at the supermarket, and it's there.
8 *Listen / Don't listen* to your brother. He's wrong.

9 ★★☆ Mick and Josh are looking for a sports shop. Complete the dialogue with the words from the list.

go | listen to | look | open | sit down | turn

Mick Where's the sports shop?
Josh OK, 0 _____sit down_____ on this chair and 1 _____ at the map.
Mick I haven't got a map.
Josh Oh, well I've got an app.
Mick Well 2 _____ the app on your phone, then.
Josh OK, OK. Wait a minute. Oh! Look, there's the sports shop. 3 _____ down here and 4 _____ left. The sports shop is behind the chemist.
Mick Is it opposite the phone shop?
Josh No, 5 _____ me, Mick! It's on the corner, behind the chemist.

GET IT RIGHT!

some and *any*

We use *some* in affirmative sentences and *any* in negative sentences.

✓ I've got some time.
✗ I've got any time.
✓ He hasn't got any money.
✗ He hasn't got some money.

Complete the sentences with *some* or *any*.

0 I haven't got _____any_____ pets.
1 There are _____ good games.
2 Don't bring _____ food.
3 They haven't got _____ homework.
4 I have _____ time.
5 I have _____ presents for you.
6 We don't have _____ problems.

🔤 VOCABULARY
Places in a town/city
→ SB p.40

1 ⭐⭐☆ **Where are these people? Write a word from the list.**

> bank | chemist | library | museum | park
> ~~post office~~ | restaurant | supermarket | train station

0 Hi. This letter to Australia, please.
_____*post office*_____

1 We need some apples and bananas.
_____

2 Look! These paintings are 200 years old!
_____

3 A return ticket to Cambridge, please.
_____

4 Please be quiet in here. People are reading.
_____

5 It's a great day for a picnic here.
_____

6 Hi. Can I change these dollars for pounds, please?
_____

7 The steak and salad for me, please.
_____

8 I need some medicine for my eye.
_____

Prepositions of place
→ SB p.41

2 ⭐☆☆ **Look at the map of the shopping centre and circle the correct option.**

cinema

0 The electronics shop is *behind* / *next to* the bank.
1 The electronics shop is *between* / *in front of* the bank and the bookshop.
2 The bookshop is *opposite* / *on the corner*.
3 The shoe shop is *between* / *opposite* the supermarket.
4 The bank is *next to* / *behind* the shoe shop.
5 The café is *behind* / *in front of* the cinema.

PRONUNCIATION
Word stress in numbers **Go to page 119.**

---

3 ⭐⭐☆ **Look at the map again. Use the prepositions in Exercise 2 to complete the sentences.**

0 The chemist is _____*next to*_____ the supermarket.
1 The restaurant is _____ the shoe shop.
2 The post office is _____ the restaurant and the phone shop.
3 The restaurant is _____ the supermarket.
4 The sports shop is _____ the chemist.
5 The cinema is _____ the café.
6 The phone shop is _____ the bookshop.

Numbers 100+
→ SB p.42

4 ⭐☆☆ **Write the words or numbers.**

0 ___110___ _*One hundred and ten*_
1 _____ one hundred and seventeen
2 125 _____
3 _____ one hundred and ninety-eight
4 215 _____
5 _____ three hundred and twelve
6 652 _____
7 _____ one thousand three hundred
8 1,400 _____
9 _____ two thousand six hundred and twenty

Prices
→ SB p.43

5 ⭐⭐☆ **Write the prices in words.**

0 _*twelve dollars fifty*_   **3** _____

1 _____   **4** _____

2 _____   **5** _____

6 ⭐⭐⭐ **Write the name of places/things you know.**

1 a famous tower   _____
2 a good shoe shop   _____
3 a famous square   _____
4 a statue of a famous person _____
5 a famous palace   _____

REFERENCE

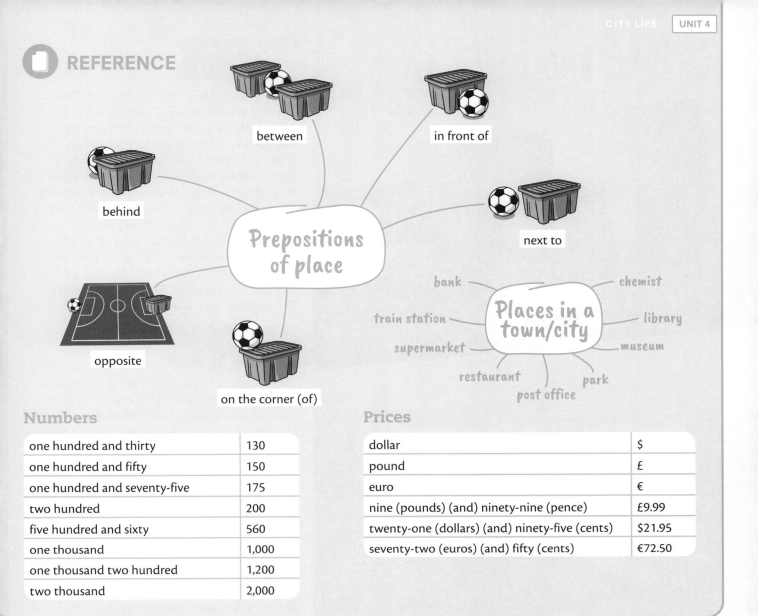

between

in front of

behind

Prepositions of place

next to

opposite

on the corner (of)

Places in a town/city

bank
chemist.
train station
library
supermarket
museum
restaurant
park
post office

Numbers

one hundred and thirty	130
one hundred and fifty	150
one hundred and seventy-five	175
two hundred	200
five hundred and sixty	560
one thousand	1,000
one thousand two hundred	1,200
two thousand	2,000

Prices

dollar	$
pound	£
euro	€
nine (pounds) (and) ninety-nine (pence)	£9.99
twenty-one (dollars) (and) ninety-five (cents)	$21.95
seventy-two (euros) (and) fifty (cents)	€72.50

VOCABULARY *EXTRA*

1 **Put the name of a place in town from the list under the pictures.**

bus station | car park | police station | skate park | ~~theatre~~

0 _theatre_   1 _____   2 _____   3 _____   4 _____

2 **Match the signs with the places from Exercise 1.**

A _____
B _____
C _____
D _____
E _____

COME AND LIVE IN ...

CALGARY

Calgary is a city of 1.3 million people in Canada. It is next to two rivers and near the Rocky Mountains. It's a clean and friendly place to live. Calgary is usually warm, dry and very sunny in summer, but there is lots of snow in winter. Many people who live in Calgary come from other Canadian cities and other countries. There are lots of places to see plays and hear live music. Country music is very popular. There are a lot of cafés and restaurants with food from all over the world. Lots of people like skiing, too. Near Calgary is the famous Banff National Park, with the beautiful Lake Louise. This fantastic park is in the Rocky Mountains.

MONTREAL

Montreal, in the Quebec province on the east coast, is Canada's second biggest city. Around 1.8 million people live here. French is the official language, but most people speak English, too. The city is on an island between the St Lawrence and Ottawa rivers, close to the sea. Winter in Montreal is very cold (-20°C) and long. There is usually snow from December to March. Montreal has 35 kilometres of tunnels under the city. So, when it is cold, people can walk to stations, shopping centres, offices, banks, and many other buildings. The summer is short and warm, and there are some beautiful beaches near the city. There are lots of exciting things to do in the city. You can go and eat in one of the excellent restaurants. In July there is a big international jazz festival.

READING

1 Read the text about two Canadian cities quickly. Which city is the biggest?

2 Read the texts again. Mark the sentences C (Calgary), M (Montreal) or B (both cities).

0 It's in Canada. [B]
1 It's near the mountains. ☐
2 It's on the coast. ☐
3 Two rivers pass the city. ☐
4 A lot of people speak two languages. ☐
5 It's very cold for four months or more. ☐
6 It's warm and dry a lot of the year. ☐
7 There are lots of restaurants. ☐
8 Many people enjoy winter sports. ☐
9 There is an unusual travel system. ☐
10 People here like country music. ☐

3 CRITICAL THINKING Read what these people say. Are they in Calgary or Montreal? Write the name of the correct city.

1 The National Park is only 90 minutes by car.
_____

2 The festival has people from all over the world. I love it! _____

3 We go to the beach after school sometimes.
_____

4 Everyone here is very friendly. _____

5 It's cold outside, but I can walk to my office underground. _____

DEVELOPING *Writing*

Your town/city

1 INPUT **Read the text. Does Laurent like weekends in his town?**

A weekend in my town

I live in Béziers, in the south of France. I like my town. It isn't very big, but the people here are nice.

At the weekend, there are lots of things to do. The town centre is small, but there are some nice shops and cafés, so I go into the centre on Saturday afternoon to meet my friends. We have lunch together, or we do some shopping. Some days, we don't buy anything, but it's always fun.

There's a cinema in the town, too, so on Friday or Saturday night, my friends and I see a film together. I like volleyball, so on Sunday morning I play with lots of friends in the park. There are three volleyball courts in the park. It's really good.

Not far from the town there's a river. It's great to swim there, but only in the summer!

My town is OK and my friends are great, so the weekends here are not bad.

2 ANALYSE **Complete the sentences with *or, and* or *so*.**

1 On Saturday evening we go to the cinema _____ we see a film.
2 Do you want to play football _____ volleyball?
3 My cousins live 300 kilometres away, _____ I don't visit them very often.

3 Match the words (1–3) with the phrases (a–c).

1 in   a the weekend
2 on   b the summer
3 at   c Sunday morning

4 PLAN **Think about a weekend in your town/city. What do you do? Use the ideas below to make notes.**

What I do on Saturday _____
_____
What I do on Sunday _____
_____
What I do with my friends _____
_____
What we do in the summer _____
_____
What we do in the winter _____
_____

5 PRODUCE **Use your notes and the text about Béziers to write a text about weekends where you live. Write about 50 words.**

_____
_____
_____
_____
_____
_____
_____
_____
_____
_____
_____
_____

✏ **WRITING TIP: Connecting things**

When writing your text, it's a good idea to use *and, or,* and *so* to join connected ideas together. For example:

We have a drink and a snack together, or we do some shopping.
I like volleyball, so on Sunday morning I play with friends in the park.

🎧 LISTENING

1 🔊 4.02 **Listen to Stella and Max talking to their Aunt Mary. Tick (✓) the places they talk about.**

bank ☐ | bookshop ✓ | café ☐ chemist ☐
library ☐ | museum ☐ park ☐ | post office ☐
shopping centre ☐ | station ☐ | supermarket ☐

2 🔊 4.02 **Listen again and correct the sentences.**

0 There isn't a good shopping centre.
  There's a good shopping centre.

1 The museum is on Grand Parade.
  _____

2 The museum is very big.
  _____

3 The shopping centre is next to the museum.
  _____

4 Max wants some pens and pencils for his project.
  _____

5 There aren't any cafés in the shopping centre.
  _____

6 Aunt Mary's favourite café is next to the bookshop.
  _____

DIALOGUE

3 **Bea is in a clothes shop. Put the conversation in order.**

☐ **Woman** £15.50.

☐ **Woman** OK. That's £31.00, please.

☐ **Woman** Hello. Can I help you?

☐ **Woman** Yes. There's this one here.

☐ **Bea** Hi. Yes. Have you got any yellow T-shirts?

☐ **Bea** Great! I'd like two, please.

☐ **Bea** Oh, it's really nice. How much is it?

4 **Complete the conversation with words and phrases from the list.**

can | expensive | is | much | that's | three

Man 0 ___*Can*___ I help you?

Matteo Yes, have you got any postcards?

Man Yes, there are 1_____ different postcards.

Matteo How 2_____ are they?

Man They're £1.50 each.

Matteo OK, three, please.

Man That's £4.50.

Matteo And how much 3_____ that small book about the museum?

Man It's £5.70.

Matteo And that big book?

Man That's £25.00.

Matteo That's very 4_____ . Just the cards and the small book.

Man OK. 5_____ £10.20.

5 **Imagine you're in a bookshop. Write a conversation similar to the one in Exercise 3.**

_____
_____
_____
_____
_____
_____
_____
_____
_____
_____
_____
_____
_____

Train to TH!NK

Exploring numbers

6 **Seth and Ari want to buy things for their room at home. They have £300. They buy five things and they have £35 left. Tick (✓) what they buy.**

armchair – £60 ☐
VR headset – £50 ☐
chair – £20 ☐
desk – £30 ☐
smart speakers – £25 ☐
table – £35 ☐
TV – £100 ☐

EXAM SKILLS: LISTENING
Identifying text type

1 🔊 **4.03** **Listen to the three conversations. How many people are speaking in each conversation?**

Conversation 1: _____

Conversation 2: _____

Conversation 3: _____

2 **Match the descriptions with the pictures. Write 1–3 in the boxes.**

   1 a news report on TV

   2 an announcement at a train station

   3 people in a shop

B ☐

A ☐

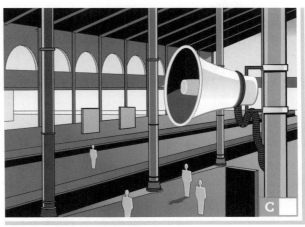

C ☐

3 🔊 **4.03** **Listen again. Match the situations with the pictures. Write A–C in the boxes.**

Conversation 1 ➜ picture ☐

Conversation 2 ➜ picture ☐

Conversation 3 ➜ picture ☐

🎧 LISTENING TIP

When you listen to a text for the first time, you don't need to understand every word. Listen to the important things:

- the number of speakers
- sounds and noises to tell you where the speakers are
- the way the speakers talk, e.g. are they happy, angry, worried, sad, excited, bored or none of these?
- 'important' words – read the question first and think of words (nouns, adjectives or verbs) that might help you to answer it. These are the 'important' words to listen for.

4 🔊 **4.03** **Listen again to the three conversations. Which words in Exercise 3 helped you decide?**

Conversation 1: _____

Conversation 2: _____

Conversation 3: _____

CONSOLIDATION

🎧 LISTENING

1 🔊 4.04 **Listen to Joaquin talking about his family and where they live. Circle the correct answers (A, B or C).**

1 How many people are there in Joaquin's family?

   A six   **B** eight   **C** ten

2 How many sisters has Joaquin got?

   A four   **B** five   **C** six

3 Where is Joaquin from?

   A the US   **B** France   **C** Italy

4 What's his cousin called?

   A Leo   **B** Javi   **C** Petra

2 🔊 4.04 **Listen again. How many are there? Write the numbers in the boxes.**

 A ☐

 D ☐

 B ☐

 E ☐

 C ☐

 F ☐

🔤 VOCABULARY

3 **Match the words in A with the words in B to make pairs.**

A

| bathroom | brother | garage | husband kitchen | living room | son | uncle |

B

| aunt | car | cooker | daughter shower | sister | sofa | wife |

0 *bathroom – shower*

1 _____

2 _____

3 _____

4 _____

5 _____

6 _____

7 _____

4 **Write the names of the shops and the prices.**

0

Chemist – it's three pounds twenty-nine.

£3.29

1

_____

_____

$14.99

2

_____

_____

€2.50

3

_____

_____

€79.59

4

_____

_____

£12.99

44

⊚ GRAMMAR

5 **Complete the sentences with words from the list. There are two extra words.**

> any | her | his | is | some | their | those | turn

1 Ask Luke. It's _____ sandwich.
2 There _____ a big park near my house.
3 Paul is Danny and Olivia's brother. He's _____ brother.
4 The shoe shop? OK, just _____ right on the High Street and it's there.
5 There aren't _____ parks near here.
6 Can I see _____ trousers in the window, please?

DIALOGUE

6 **◁)) 4.05** **Complete the conversation with words from the list. Then listen and check.**

> looks | much | really | right | thank | what

Jordan I like your T-shirt, Rachel.
Rachel ¹_____ ? It's very old.
Jordan Well, I think it ²_____ cool. And ³_____ a great hat, too.
Rachel ⁴_____ you. It's new.
Jordan How ⁵_____ was it?
Rachel Well, it was a present from my mum.
Jordan Oh, ⁶_____ . I'll ask her, then.

📖 READING

7 **Read the conversation and complete the sentences.**

Woman Hello, can I help you?
Ahmet Yes, I'd like to see those hats behind you.
Woman The black ones for teenagers?
Ahmet No, the red ones next to them.
Woman OK. Yes, these are really popular. Here you are.
Ahmet How much are they?
Woman Wait a minute. Let me see. They're £5.99.
Ahmet OK, great! Can I have three, please?
Woman Wow! You really like them.
Ahmet They're not for me. They're for my sisters.

Woman Your sisters?
Ahmet Yes, it's their birthday tomorrow. They're nine.
Woman So they're triplets?
Ahmet Yes, all three were born on the same day.
Woman Is it difficult? I mean, having three sisters?
Ahmet Three? There's three more as well.
Woman Six sisters? Poor you! Here, have a black hat. It's for you.
Ahmet Wow, thanks. That's really kind!

1 Ahmet wants to see the _____ hats.
2 The hats are _____ each.
3 The hats are for his _____ .
4 It's their _____ tomorrow.
5 Triplets are _____ children born on the same day.
6 Ahmet has _____ sisters.
7 The woman gives Ahmet a free _____ .
8 Ahmet thinks the woman is very _____ .

✏️ WRITING

8 **Write a short text about your family and where you live. Write about 50 words. Use the questions to help you.**

• Who is in your family?
• What is your house like?
• What is your town like?

Grammar rap!

GRAMMAR
Present simple
→ SB p.50

1 ★☆☆ (Circle) the correct options.

0 I (play) / plays tennis every day.
1 My cousins *speak / speaks* Spanish.
2 Mr Clark *teach / teaches* History.
3 The dog *like / likes* the park.
4 We sometimes *go / goes* to bed very late.
5 You *live / lives* near me.

2 ★★☆ Complete the sentences with the present simple form of the verbs in brackets. Which four sentences match the pictures? Write the numbers in the boxes.

0 My dad ____*flies*____ planes. (fly)
1 The boys _____ a lot of video games. (play)
2 Miss Dawson _____ technology. (teach)
3 Nina _____ in the library every day. (study)
4 Emili and Dana _____ the guitar. (play)
5 Mum _____ gardens. (love)

 A
 C
 B
 D

3 ★★☆ Complete the sentences with the correct form of the verbs in the list.

finish | go | like | play | speak
study | teach | watch

0 Mum ____*likes*____ pop music.
1 My father _____ Maths at my school.
2 Lucia _____ to a drama club on Wednesdays.
3 Yunus _____ four languages. He's amazing.
4 My brother _____ TV after school.
5 Our school _____ at 3.15 pm.
6 Gianna _____ the piano every afternoon.
7 My sister _____ every weekend.

PRONUNCIATION
Present simple verbs – third person
Go to page 119. 🎧

Adverbs of frequency
→ SB p.50

4 ★☆☆ Put the adverbs in the correct order on the line.

often | always | sometimes | never

1 _____ 2 _____ 3 _____ 4 _____

5 ★★☆ Write the sentences with the adverb of frequency in the correct place.

0 I meet my friends in town on Saturdays. (sometimes)
I sometimes meet my friends in town on Saturdays.
1 Jennie is happy. (always)
_____
2 They do homework at the weekend. (never)
_____
3 You help Mum and Dad make dinner. (sometimes)
_____
4 We are tired on Friday evenings. (often)
_____
5 It rains on Sundays! (always)
_____
6 Mum flies to Paris for work. (often)
_____
7 I am bored at the weekend. (never)
_____

6 ★★★ **Write sentences so they are true for you. Use adverbs of frequency.**

1 do homework after school
_____

2 play computer games at the weekend
_____

3 watch TV on Sunday afternoons
_____

4 listen to music in the morning
_____

5 text my best friend in the evening
_____

Present simple (negative)   → SB p.51

7 ★★☆ **Complete the sentences with the negative form of the verbs in brackets.**

0 My mum ___doesn't write___ books for children. (write)
1 I _____ to music lessons after school. (go)
2 My cousins _____ to a lot of music. (listen)
3 My grandfather _____ model planes. (make)
4 We _____ games on our tablet. (play)
5 School _____ at 8.00 am. (start)
6 My sister _____ singing or dancing. (like)
7 You _____ in a small house. (live)

8 ★★☆ **Match these sentences with the sentences from Exercise 7.**

[0] She writes for teenagers.
a ☐ It's really big.
b ☐ But the gates open at that time.
c ☐ We play them on the computer.
d ☐ She's quite shy.
e ☐ I go to them on Saturdays.
f ☐ He makes trains.
g ☐ But they watch a lot of TV.

Present simple (questions)   → SB p.52

9 ★☆☆ **Complete the questions with Do or Does.**

0 ___Do___ you live in Sydney?
1 _____ Pablo like sport?
2 _____ you know the answer?
3 _____ your sister play tennis?
4 _____ you often go to the cinema?
5 _____ your teacher give you a lot of homework?

10 ★★★ **Write the questions. Then write answers so they are true for you.**

0 your mother / speak English?
Does your mother speak English?
Yes, she does.

1 you / always do your homework?
_____
_____

2 your best friend / play the piano?
_____
_____

3 you / sometimes play computer games before school?
_____
_____

4 you and your friends / play basketball?
_____
_____

5 your mum / drive a big car?
_____
_____

GET IT RIGHT!

Adverbs of frequency

With the verb *to be*, we use this word order: subject + verb + adverb of frequency. With other verbs, we use this word order: subject + adverb of frequency + verb.

✓ He is always friendly.
✗ He always is friendly.
✓ I often watch football on TV.
✗ I watch often football on TV.

Circle the correct sentences.

0 a I eat often ice cream.
  b (I often eat ice cream.)
1 a I play often computer games.
  b I often play computer games.
2 a I always go to the cinema with my friends.
  b Always I go to the cinema with my friends.
3 a That singer is always great.
  b That singer always is great.
4 a I ride a bike in the park never.
  b I never ride a bike in the park.
5 a I sometimes am bored.
  b I am sometimes bored.

VOCABULARY
Free-time activities

→ SB p.50

1 ⭐☆☆ **Match the parts of the sentences.**

0 I play ⬜ *e*
1 I go ⬜
2 I hang out with ⬜
3 I chat ⬜
4 I listen to ⬜
5 I dance ⬜

a shopping with Mum on Saturdays.
b to Suki online all the time.
c music in bed.
d to rock music with my friends.
e computer games on my tablet.
f my friends in the park after school.

2 ⭐⭐☆ **Complete the sentences with words from the list.**

> dance | homework | listens
> out | plays | shopping

0 Every day after school I hang ___*out*___ at the sports club.
1 Siena goes _____ with her sister on Saturday afternoons.
2 Toni never does his _____ on time.
3 We _____ every weekend at the kids' disco.
4 My brother _____ computer games all weekend!
5 My dad _____ to really old music.

3 ⭐⭐⭐ **Write sentences that are true for you. Use adverbs of frequency.**

1 play computer games
_____

2 go shopping
_____

3 dance
_____

4 chat to friends online
_____

5 listen to music
_____

6 hang out with friends
_____

7 do homework
_____

8 go to the cinema
_____

Gadgets

→ SB p.53

4 ⭐⭐☆ **Put the letters in order to make words for gadgets.**

0 blteat   ___*tablet*___
1 megas loscone   _____
2 RV stheeda   _____
3 marsthopen   _____
4 ahehndspoe   _____
5 SGP   _____
6 plapto   _____
7 ard-eere   _____

5 ⭐⭐⭐ **Answer the questions so they are true for you.**

1 What do you use to play computer games?
_____

2 What do you use to listen to music?
_____

3 What do you use to find your way?
_____

4 What do you use to read books, magazines or comics?
_____

Days in your life

→ SB p.53

6 ⭐⭐☆ **Complete the days of the week with the missing letters. Then put the days in order.**

0 *M o* nday   1 _____
1 __ __dnesday   2 _____
2 __ __iday   3 _____
3 __ __esday   4 _____
4 __ __nday   5 _____
5 __ __ursday   6 _____
6 __ __turday   7 _____

7 ⭐⭐⭐ **Choose three days. Write sentences so they are true for you.**

I love Fridays because I always go to the cinema with my dad in the evening.
_____
_____
_____
_____
_____
_____
_____
_____
_____

REFERENCE
Free-time activities

play computer games

dance

hang out with friends

go shopping

do homework

chat to friends online

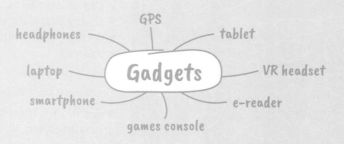

GPS
headphones
tablet
laptop
Gadgets
VR headset
smartphone
e-reader
games console

Days of the week

Monday	Tuesday	Wednesday	Thursday	Friday	Saturday	Sunday

VOCABULARY *EXTRA*

1   **Where do people usually do these activities? Tick (✓) the correct column.**

	indoors	outdoors
1 ride your bike	☐	☐
2 play board games	☐	☐
3 read comics	☐	☐
4 watch videos online	☐	☐
5 roller-skate	☐	☐

2   **Complete the sentences so they are true for you. Use the activities from Exercise 1.**

1   I often _____ after school.

2   I never _____ in the mornings.

3   I always _____ at the weekend.

4   I never _____ when I'm tired.

5   I sometimes _____ with my mum/dad.

3   **Answer the questions about the activities from Exercise 1.**

1   Which do you really like?

_____

2   Which do you often do?

_____

3   Which do you never do?

_____

49

Computer gaming club

Come and get better at all your favourite games. Learn from your friends and show them what you know. Mrs Stephens also shows you how to make your own simple games.
A _____

Years 7 and 8 – Tuesday lunchtime in Room 4

Dance club

Join Mr Roberts for an hour of exercise and have loads of fun at the same time. Learn how to dance to all the best modern pop songs. And it's not just for students at the school – anyone is welcome!
C _____

All years – Wednesday lunchtime in the school gym

HOMEWORK CLUB

Don't do all of your homework after school or at weekends. Come to Homework Club and do it all before you go home. There's always a teacher here to help you if you have a problem, so when you get home after school you can have fun! B _____

All years – every day after school in Room 8

FILM CLUB

Watch classic films from the 1980s and 1990s: *E.T.*, *Toy Story*, *Jurassic Park*, etc. Then talk about them with Miss Owens and other students.
D _____

Bring your own popcorn!

Years 9–11 – Thursday after school in Room 14

📖 READING

1 Look at the pictures and read the messages. Write the rooms and the names of the clubs.

1 _____
_____

3 _____
_____

2 _____
_____

4 _____
_____

2 Match the sentences or phrases with the correct places (A–D) in the messages.

0 Tell your parents homework finishes at 5pm. ☐ B

1 Wear comfortable clothes! ☐

2 It's great for all students who love gadgets. ☐

3 Ask your parents about some of their favourites, and we can add them to the list. ☐

3 CRITICAL THINKING **Answer the questions. Write sentences.**

1 Which club do you like? Why?

_____
_____

2 Which club don't you like? Why?

_____
_____

3 Think of one more club to add. What can kids do there? When and where is it?

_____
_____
_____

DEVELOPING Writing

My week

1 **INPUT** **Read the text. On which day does Lucia not do any homework?**

Lucia's Busy Life

A typical week ...

Posted: **MONDAY 10 APRIL**

From Monday to Friday, I go to school from 9 am to 3 pm every day. But my day doesn't finish then!

After school on Mondays, I have violin lessons from 4 pm to 5 pm. In the evenings, I do my homework.

On Tuesdays and Thursdays, I go to karate class from 4 pm to 6 pm. In the evenings, I do my homework.

On Wednesday afternoons, I go to gaming club from 3 pm to 4 pm. And in the evenings? Yep, I do my homework.

On Fridays, I do my homework after school! I go to coding club in the evenings. It finishes at 9 pm.

On Saturdays, I do things with Mum and Dad. We go shopping or visit Grandma. My dad sometimes takes us to watch football.

On Sundays, I sleep! Oh, and then I do some homework.

2 **ANALYSE** **Complete the sentences with the correct prepositions. Use the text in Exercise 1 to help you.**

1 I play tennis _____ Tuesdays and Thursdays. I play _____ 4 pm _____ 6 pm.
2 _____ Wednesday afternoons I go to dance club. It starts _____ 3 pm and finishes _____ 4 pm.
3 _____ Monday to Friday I go to school.

3 **Match the parts of the phrases. Then check your answers in the text in Exercise 1.**

1 do   a a piano lesson
2 go   b to dance club / shopping
3 have   c homework

4 **PLAN** **Think about your typical week. Use the questions to make notes.**

What do you do during the day? Which days are different?
_____

What do you do after school? What days do you do things on?
_____

What do you do in the evenings?
_____

What do you do at the weekend?
_____

WRITING TIP: Prepositions

When you write about your week, be careful to use the correct preposition:
- *IN* the evening
- *ON* Monday evening / Saturday
- *AT* the weekend

5 **PRODUCE** **Use your notes and the sentences below to write a text about a typical week for you. Write about 50 words.**

_____
_____
_____
_____
_____
_____
_____
_____
_____
_____

LISTENING

1 🔊 **5.02** **Listen to Rahul and Prisha talking about a competition. Circle the correct option in each sentence.**

0 Prisha feels *worried* / *excited* about the competition.

1 She doesn't like *her team* / *people watching her*.

2 The competition is in *a museum* / *the robotics club*.

3 Rahul says Prisha forgets her *team* / *everything* else when she makes robots.

4 Rahul offers to come to the robotics club *with his friends* / *on his own*.

5 Prisha thinks this is *a good idea* / *not necessary*.

2 🔊 **5.02** **Listen again and underline the incorrect information in the sentences. Then write the correct information.**

0 Prisha is in a <u>drama</u> competition.

*robotics*_____

1 Prisha doesn't like making robots.

_____

2 In the team they don't work together.

_____

3 The competition is in the Natural History Museum.

_____

4 Robotics club is on Monday and Wednesday.

_____

5 Prisha doesn't want Rahul to come to robotics club.

_____

DIALOGUE

3 **Complete the conversation with the phrases from the list.**

> don't worry | here to help you | No problem
> You can do it | ~~you're good~~

Prisha ... And I don't like that.

Rahul Oh, I see. But your team is the best in our school, and ⁰____*you're good*____ !

Prisha Hmm, do you think so?

Rahul Yes! So, come on. ¹_____ , Prisha.

Prisha Really?

Rahul Yes, of course! And I'm ²_____ .

Prisha You are? How?

Rahul Is the Robotics club on Thursday?

Prisha Yes, Monday and Thursday lunchtimes.

Rahul OK, so ³_____ ! Next time, I'm there with my friends to watch you!

Prisha Oh, thanks, Rahul. You're a really good friend!

Rahul ⁴_____ ! I want you to win.

4 **Look at the picture and write a short conversation. Use phrases from Exercise 3.**

PHRASES FOR FLUENCY
→ SB p.54

5 **Match the sentences.**

0 What's wrong? — d

1 I've got an idea. ☐

2 Ana, do you want to be in the school football team? ☐

3 I don't want to play football. ☐

a Really. What is it?

b No way!

c Oh, come on. We really need you.

d I feel a bit ill.

6 **Use two of the pairs of sentences in Exercise 5 to complete the conversations.**

Conversation 1

George _____

Sara _____

George But I hate football. And I'm terrible at it.

Sara No, you're not. You're great.

Conversation 2

Abi I'm sorry, Simon. I don't really want to go shopping.

Simon _____

Abi _____

Simon Oh, dear. Let me get you a glass of water.

7 **Use the other two pairs of sentences in Exercise 5 to make your own conversations.**

SUM IT UP

1   **This is Millie's diary. Make sentences about her week.**

0   *On Monday, she goes to dance class.*

1 _____

2 _____

3 _____

4 _____

5 _____

Monday	dance class
Tuesday	roller-skating
Wednesday	shopping for comics
Thursday	computer games
Friday	friends
Saturday	music
Sunday	sleep

2   **Use the code to work out the message.**

CODE

● = a	✳ = b	⇒ = c	■ = d
✜ = e	❀ = f	✓ = g	★ = h
✂ = i	▶ = j	◗ = k	♣ = l
♥ = m	☎ = n	☞ = o	→ = p
♠ = q	◆ = r	✳ = s	✪ = t
✏ = u	○ = v	❀ = w	➤ = x
☆ = y	❖ = z		

3   **What do you want for your birthday? Use the code to write your own message.**

_____

_____

Grammar rap! ▶17

ⓖ GRAMMAR

have / has got
(positive and negative) → SB p.58

1 ★☆☆ Circle the correct options.

0 I *has got* / *have got* a new friend.

1 My friend Samira *has got* / *have got* a tablet.

2 Luna *has got* / *have got* a big family.

3 We *has got* / *have got* a cat.

4 All of my friends *has got* / *have got* bikes.

2 ★★☆ **Look at the table and complete the sentences.**

has / hasn't got	Sally	Tom	Dan	Elif
smartphone	✓	✗	✓	✗
laptop	✗	✗	✗	✗
bike	✓	✗	✓	✓
games console	✗	✓	✗	✗
cat	✓	✓	✓	✓

0 Tom _____*hasn't got*_____ a smartphone.

1 Sally _____ a laptop or a games console.

2 Dan and Elif _____ a bike.

3 Tom _____ a games console.

4 All of them _____ a cat.

5 Tom and Dan _____ a laptop.

3 ★★★ **Write sentences so they are true for you. Use *have got* or *haven't got* and phrases from the list.**

> a big family | a pet | a new smartphone
> a sister | a tablet | black hair | brown eyes
> three brothers

1 _____

2 _____

3 _____

4 _____

5 _____

6 _____

7 _____

8 _____

4 ★★★ **Write sentences under the photos. Use phrases from the list and *have got* or *has got*.**

> a shaved head | long curly hair
> long straight hair | short curly hair

_____

_____

have / has got (questions) → SB p.59

5 ★☆☆ Circle the correct options.

1 A *Have* / *Has* you got your own laptop?

   B No, I *haven't* / *hasn't*. But my big brother has got one.

2 A *Have* / *Has* Katya got a Little Mix poster?

   B No, she *haven't* / *hasn't*. She doesn't like them.

3 A *Have* / *Has* Dario and Alexei got new games consoles?

   B No, they *haven't* / *hasn't*. But I *have* / *has* got one.

4 A *Have* / *Has* you got lots of songs on your mobile?

   B Yes, I *have* / *has*. I've got thousands. I listen to them all the time.

5 A *Have* / *Has* you got bikes?

   B Yes, we *have* / *has*. We've both got bikes. We ride to school every day.

6 A *Have* / *Has* Berat got a sister?

   B No, he *haven't* / *hasn't*. He's got a brother.

6 ★★☆ **Complete the dialogue with the correct form of have got.**

Amy ⁰___Has___ your mum ___got___ brown hair?

Marco No, she ¹_____ . She ²_____ black hair.

Amy ³_____ she _____ blue eyes?

Marco No, she ⁴_____ . She ⁵_____ green eyes.

Amy ⁶_____ she _____ a daughter?

Marco No, she ⁷_____ . She ⁸_____ . one son – me!

7 ★★★ **Complete the dialogue about a member of your family.**

Friend Has he/she got green eyes?

You ¹_____

Friend Has he/she got a big family?

You ²_____

Friend Has he/she got a car?

You ³_____

Friend Has he/she got a dog?

You ⁴_____

Friend Has he/she got a smartphone?

You ⁵_____

Countable and uncountable nouns

→ SB p.59

8 ★☆☆ **Write C (countable) or U (uncountable).**

0 chair ☐ C
1 nose ☐
2 cat ☐
3 fun ☐
4 friend ☐
5 time ☐
6 work ☐
7 hospital ☐
8 name ☐
9 teacher ☐

9 Circle **the correct options.**

0 It's the weekend. Let's have *a /* (*some*) fun.
1 I've got *a / some* sandwiches. I'm hungry. Let's eat one.
2 Let's listen to *a / some* music on your smartphone.
3 Marie's got *a / some* red bike.
4 I've got *a / some* money. Let's buy an ice cream.
5 He's got *a / some* hobby – painting!
6 My dad's got *a / some* work to do.
7 Murat hasn't got *an / some* apple. He's got *a / some* banana.

10 **Complete the dialogues with *a, an* or *some*.**

1 **A** Would you like ___some___ ice cream?
   B No, thanks. I've got _____ apple.
2 **A** Have you got _____ hobby?
   B Yes, I have. I sing in a band.
3 **A** Have you got _____ best friend?
   B Yes, I have. Her name's Zeynep.
4 **A** I've got _____ money from my mum.
   B Me, too!
   A That's good. Let's buy _____ sweets.
5 **A** I haven't got a pen.
   B Oh, I've got _____ . I've got blue, black and red. Is that OK?
   A Yes, perfect!

GET IT RIGHT!

Countable and uncountable nouns

We add *-s* to the end of countable nouns to make them plural, but not to uncountable nouns.

✓ *I've got a lot of friends.*
✗ *I've got a lot of friend.*
✓ *I drink a lot of water.*
✗ *I drink a lot of waters.*

Circle **the correct options.**

0 How many *pen /* (*pens*) has he got?
1 I listen to *musics / music* in my bedroom.
2 They've got a lot of *hobby / hobbies*.
3 Have you got enough *money / moneys* for your lunch?
4 Homework isn't always a lot of *fun / funs*.
5 Her brother has got two *phone / phones*.
6 This street has got a lot of *shop / shops*.

 **VOCABULARY**
Parts of the body

→ SB p.58

1 ⭐☆☆ **Complete the sentences and the crossword with the same words.**

[crossword grid]

ACROSS

1 You hug with your _____ .

6 You kick with your _____ .

7 You hold with your _____ .

8 You hear with your _____ .

DOWN

2 You eat with your _____ .

3 You walk with your _____ .

4 You smell with your _____ .

5 You see with your _____ .

Describing people (1)

→ SB p.60

2 ⭐⭐☆ **Circle the correct options.**

0 His hair isn't curly. It's *wavy* / brown.

1 She's got *short / blonde* red hair.

2 Her eyes are *straight / green*.

3 My mother always wears her hair *straight / brown* for work.

4 The old man has grey *curly / hair*.

5 His hair *colour / style* is black.

Describing people (2)

→ SB p.61

3 ⭐☆☆ **Complete the words with *a, e, i, o* or *u*.**

0 m _o_ _u_ st _a_ ch _e_

1 gl __ ss __ s

2 t __ ll

3 b __ __ rd

4 sm __ l __

5 __ __ r r __ ngs

6 sh __ rt

4 ⭐☆☆ **Match the words with the things in the picture. Write 1–6 in the boxes.**

Seline | Mr Chips | Arturo

Katy

1 beard | 2 earrings | 3 glasses
4 moustache | 5 wavy

5 ⭐⭐☆ **Look at the picture and write the names of the people.**

0 She's got earrings. _____Seline_____

1 He's got a very big moustache. _____

2 She's got a lovely smile. _____

3 He's got a very long beard. _____

4 She wears glasses. _____

6 ⭐⭐⭐ **Write one more sentence about each person from Exercise 4.**

1 _____

2 _____

3 _____

4 _____

PRONUNCIATION
Long vowel sound /eɪ/ Go to page 119.

REFERENCE

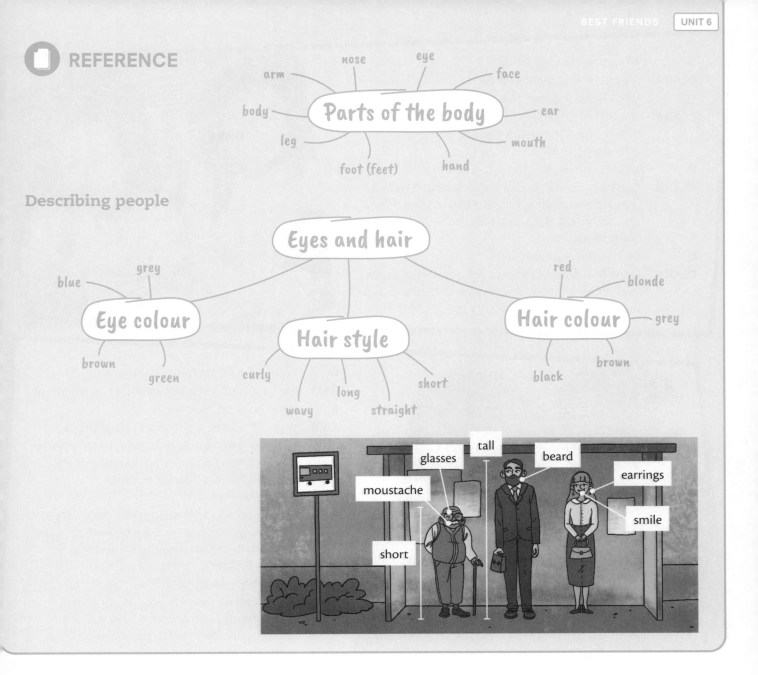

Parts of the body
- arm
- nose
- eye
- face
- body
- ear
- leg
- mouth
- foot (feet)
- hand

Describing people

Eyes and hair

Eye colour
- blue
- grey
- brown
- green

Hair style
- curly
- wavy
- long
- straight
- short

Hair colour
- red
- blonde
- grey
- brown
- black

Labels in picture: glasses, tall, beard, moustache, earrings, smile, short

VOCABULARY *EXTRA*

1 **Match the words with the pictures.**

> 1 braces | 2 plaits | 3 ponytail | 4 old | 5 young

 A
 B
 C
 D
 E

2 (Circle) the correct words.

1 A lot of teenagers have *braces* / *ponytail* on their teeth.

2 You're very *young* / *old* to go to university – you're only 16.

3 My brother has got a *plaits* / *ponytail*, but I don't like it.

4 My grandmother is very *young* / *old* but she still does a lot of sport.

5 People with long hair sometimes wear their hair in a ponytail or in *plaits* / *braces*.

Q	Who is your best friend?
CLARA	My best friend's name is Ailsa.
Q	What does she look like?
CLARA	She's very pretty. She's got curly black hair and brown eyes. She wears glasses and she's got a friendly smile.
Q	What's she like?
CLARA	She's very clever and she's very kind. She likes drawing and making things. I like making things, too. We've got the same hobbies. I think that's really important.
Q	Why is she a good friend?
CLARA	Good friends share things with you. Ailsa shares everything with me. She shares her chocolate and her clothes, too. She's a very special friend.

Q	Who is your best friend?
SAM	My best friend is a school friend called Murat.
Q	What does he look like?
SAM	He's tall and he's got short straight brown hair and green eyes. He's got a friendly smile and he laughs a lot. We play video games together. We like the same things.
Q	What's he like?
SAM	He's funny and tells good jokes. He's very good at sports, and he likes basketball. I like basketball, too. We like the same team. That's important, I think.
Q	Why is he a good friend?
SAM	I think friends listen to you. Murat always listens to me. Sometimes I have a problem and he helps me. He's a great friend.

📖 READING

1 **Read the two magazine texts about friendship and answer the questions.**

   1 Who has got green eyes? _____

   2 Who wears glasses? _____

2 **Read the texts again and answer the questions.**

   1 What colour is Ailsa's hair? _____

   2 What colour is Murat's hair? _____

   3 Who likes basketball? _____

   4 Who likes drawing? _____

   5 What do Murat and Sam like? _____

   6 What does Ailsa share with Clara? _____

3 **Who says these things about friendship? Write C (Clara) or S (Sam).**

A good friend …

   1 shares things with you. ☐

   2 likes the same team. ☐

   3 helps you. ☐

   4 has got the same hobbies. ☐

   5 tells you jokes. ☐

   6 listens to you. ☐

4   CRITICAL THINKING   **Which two things about Ailsa and which two things about Murat do you like? Write sentences.**

_____

_____

_____

_____

DEVELOPING *Writing*

Describing people in a story

1 **INPUT** Read about a singer from a story. What sports does he like?

2 **ANALYSE** Mark the sentences T (true) or F (false).

1 He's short. ☐
2 He wears glasses. ☐
3 He's got a moustache. ☐
4 He hasn't got a beard. ☐
5 He doesn't like tennis. ☐

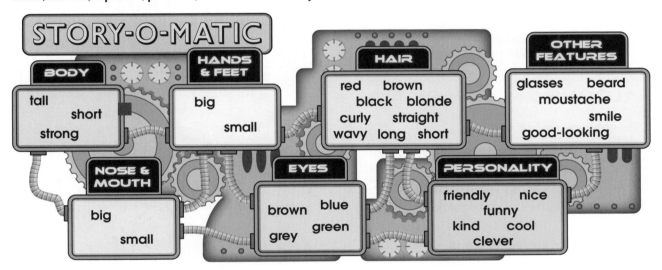

In my story, there's a singer. He's in a rock band. He's very tall. He's got short black hair and green eyes, and he wears glasses. He's got a short beard and a moustache. I think he's very good-looking. He's very active. He likes yoga and swimming, but he doesn't like tennis. He's very friendly. He's got a big smile. I think he's cool.

3 **PLAN** Think of a person from a story. He/She can be a singer, a sports person, an actor/actress, a prince/princess, etc. Choose the adjectives that describe him or her.

STORY-O-MATIC

BODY
tall
short
strong

HANDS & FEET
big
small

HAIR
red   brown
black   blonde
curly   straight
wavy   long   short

OTHER FEATURES
glasses   beard
moustache
smile
good-looking

NOSE & MOUTH
big
small

EYES
brown   blue
green
grey

PERSONALITY
friendly   nice
funny
kind   cool
clever

4 Write notes about your story person.

What does he/she look like? (hair, eyes, other features): _____
_____

Personality: _____
_____

Likes/dislikes: _____
_____

> ✎ **WRITING TIP:**
> **Using adjectives to describe people**
>
> - He/She is *tall / short*.
> - He/She has got *long / black / curly* hair.
> - He/She has got *brown / blue / green* eyes.
> - He/She has got a *black / grey / brown / long / short moustache / beard*.
> - He/She is *nice / friendly*.

5 **PRODUCE** Use your notes and the model in Exercise 1 to write a text about your story person. Write about 50 words.

_____
_____
_____
_____
_____
_____

 **LISTENING**

1 🔊 6.03 **Listen to the conversations and number the places in the order you hear them.**

a the park ☐
b a hospital ☐
c a party ☐

2 🔊 6.03 **Listen again and circle the correct options.**

1 Marcus is *tall / short* and he's got short, curly *brown / black* hair. He's got a *moustache / friendship band* and he wears *glasses / earrings*.

2 Kenzie has got a *dog / bike* with her. She's *short / tall* and she's got long, curly *brown / black* hair. She's got *brown / blue* eyes and she always wears *glasses / earrings*. She's very *funny / friendly*.

3 The nurse is *tall / short* and she's got *short / long* hair. It's *black / blonde* and it's *curly / straight*. She's got *brown / green* eyes and she's very *popular / pretty*.

DIALOGUE

3 **Put the conversation in order.**

☐ **Police officer** And what's your daughter's name?
☐ **Police officer** And what colour eyes has she got?
☐1 **Police officer** Can I take your name?
☐ **Police officer** Thank you, Mr Douglas.
☐ **Police officer** OK, first, what colour hair has she got?
☐ **Police officer** Is it long or short?
☐ **Mr Douglas** She's got dark brown hair.
☐ **Mr Douglas** My name's Neil Douglas.
☐ **Mr Douglas** She's got brown eyes and she wears glasses.
☐ **Mr Douglas** It's Ava.
☐ **Mr Douglas** It's short and curly.

Train to TH!NK

Attention to detail

4 **Spot the five differences between Picture 1 and Picture 2 and write sentences.**

Picture 1

Picture 2

0 *In picture 1, the woman has got glasses.*
   In picture 2, she hasn't got glasses.

1 _____
   _____

2 _____
   _____

3 _____
   _____

4 _____
   _____

EXAM SKILLS: WRITING
Punctuation (getting apostrophes right)

 WRITING TIP

When writing in English, it's sometimes easy to make mistakes with apostrophes ('). It's important to know when to use them and when not to use them.

- We use apostrophes to show missing letters in short forms, for example:

  He is ... ➡ *He's ...*

  She has got ... ➡ *She's got ...*

- Be careful not to confuse apostrophes for the short form of *be* and *have got* with apostrophes to show possession:

  My mum's got curly hair. (short form)

  My mum's name is Elena. (possession)

1 Complete the *Apostrophe Challenge*. Use contractions.

I think I can complete the *Apostrophe Challenge* in _____ seconds.

I am	**0** *I'm*
It is	**1**
You are	**2**
He is not	**3**
They are not	**4**
She has got	**5**
I have got	**6**
We have got	**7**
He has not got	**8**
I have not got	**9**

My time: _____ seconds.

2 Read the text. Put apostrophes in the correct places.

My best friends name is Leon. Hes 12 years old and hes in the same class as me. Leons got short, curly brown hair and green eyes. He wears glasses and hes very good-looking. Hes clever and he likes sports. Leons got a brother and a sister. Theyre eight years old and ten years old. Theyve got brown hair and blue eyes. They dont wear glasses. Leons also got a cat. Its black and white and its names Suky. Its a lovely cat.

3 Write a paragraph about one of these people. Use the questions in the box to help you.

a your best friend

b a family member

c your favourite actor/singer

- What's his/her name?
- How old is he/she?
- What does he/she look like?

_____

_____

_____

_____

_____

_____

_____

_____

_____

CONSOLIDATION

🎧 LISTENING

1 🔊 6.04 **Listen to three conversations and circle the correct answers (A, B or C).**

   1 Jonathan has got a problem with his …
      A arm.   B hand.   C leg.
   2 Maddy is …
      A nice.   B short.   C tall.
   3 How many friends has Diego got?
      A about fifty   B about fifteen   C about five

2 🔊 6.04 **Listen again and answer the questions.**

   1 What does Jonathan want to do today?
      _____
   2 What does the girl tell him to do?
      _____
   3 Does Mike know Maddy?
      _____
   4 What does Mike want Sofia to say to Maddy?
      _____
   5 When does Diego come to this place?
      _____
   6 What colour is Jack's hair?
      _____

 GRAMMAR

3 **Circle the correct options.**

   Omer   Hi Joanna. How are you? It's nice to see a friend in town.
   Joanna Hi Omer. I ¹*come always / always come* here on Saturdays.
   Omer   Do you? ²*I'm never / I never am* in town on Saturdays, usually. But it's different today because ³*I've got / I'm got* some money from babysitting.
   Joanna Great! ⁴*How much / How many* money have you got, then?
   Omer   £65.00. I ⁵*don't know / know not* what I want to buy, though. Maybe some clothes, or … .
   Joanna That's a great idea. I love clothes. I ⁶*buy / buys* new clothes every month.
   Omer   Really? So, ⁷*you got / you've got* lots of clothes at home? Can you help me, then?
   Joanna Sure! What do you need?
   Omer   Well, I'm not very good at buying clothes. Have you got ⁸*a / some* time to come with me?
   Joanna Of course. It's fun! Let's go to that shop first – ⁹*it's always got / it's got always* nice clothes.
   Omer   OK, cool. You know, Joanna, it's great to have ¹⁰*a / some* friend like you!

🔤 VOCABULARY

4 **Complete the sentences with the words in the list. There are two extra words.**

   > do | earrings | eyes | hang out | headphones
   > legs | short | smile | tall | VR headset

   1 I really like listening to rap on the bus with my
      _____ .
   2 Spiders have got eight _____ .
   3 I like Adela. She's always happy and she's got a nice
      _____ .
   4 These are my new _____ . They're very long. Do you like them?
   5 I love this _____ . It makes the games look more real.
   6 She's good at basketball because she's very
      _____ .
   7 I only _____ my homework on Sundays – never on Saturdays!
   8 On Saturdays I always _____ with my friends.

5 **Complete the words.**

   1 My favourite day of the week is F_____ .
   2 I use my t_____ every day to watch videos and play games.
   3 His hair isn't straight. It's c_____ .
   4 Let's go out on W_____ after school – to the park, maybe?
   5 My dad's got a b_____ and a moustache.
   6 His eyes aren't very good. He wears g_____ all the time.
   7 Do you want to go s_____ in the town centre tomorrow afternoon?
   8 Don't shout! Put your h_____ up if you know the answer.

DIALOGUE

6 🔊 6.05 **Complete the dialogue with words from the list. Then listen and check.**

> always | an idea | computer | haven't got | listen to | never | on | play | way | wrong

Pablo Hey, Kylie. You don't seem very happy. What's ¹_____ ?

Kylie Hi, Pablo. I'm OK. It's nothing.

Pablo Come ²_____ . Is there a problem? Tell me.

Kylie No, not really. I want to ³_____ board games tonight, but I ⁴_____ anyone to play with.

Pablo OK. Listen. I've got ⁵_____ . Let's ask Jon to come over to my house. Then we can all play some games together.

Kylie No ⁶_____ ! I don't like Jon at all. He ⁷_____ helps me or says anything nice to me. He's ⁸_____ horrible to me.

Pablo Oh, right. Then it's you and me. Two people are enough for some games.

Kylie Yes. That's true. Thanks, Pablo. So – what games have you got?

Pablo Me? Sorry, Kylie, I haven't got any board games. But I've got some ⁹_____ games. Is that OK?

Kylie No, I don't really like them! But don't worry. I can bring one or two of my board games. And we can ¹⁰_____ music at the same time, too. You've got music, haven't you?

Pablo Of course! On my phone! See you later!

📖 READING

7 **Read this text about gadgets and ⬭circle the correct answers (A or B).**

Me and my gadgets

I'm Zayn. I'm a 13-year-old boy … and I love my gadgets. I've got a tablet, a smartphone and an e-reader, and I'm always looking at one of them.

I use my tablet at home to read the football news and to chat to my friends.

I use my smartphone … well, of course, to make phone calls and to send text messages. It's good, too, when I'm on the bus. I always use it to listen to music. I've got lots of apps, too – especially apps about sport and music, because they're my favourite free-time activities.

And my e-reader? I use it to read books. I love reading and my parents and other people in my family often give me e-books to read (for my birthday, for example). I like reading before I go to sleep. I often read 20 or 30 pages at night.

1 Zayn's got …
 A three gadgets.
 B four gadgets.

2 He listens to music on …
 A his smartphone.
 B his tablet.

3 Zayn uses his smartphone to …
 A read about the news and weather.
 B talk to his friends.

4 People in Zayn's family often give him …
 A e-books for his reader.
 B pages from books to read at night.

✏️ WRITING

8 **Write a paragraph about your gadgets. Write about 50 words. Use the questions to help you.**

- What gadgets have you got?
- What do you use them for?
- When/How often do you use them?
- What gadgets do you want?

7 LIVING FOR SPORT

Grammar rap!

▶20

G GRAMMAR
can (ability)

→ SB p.68

1 ★☆☆ **Match the sentences with the pictures. Write 1–8 in the boxes.**

1 He can ride a bike.
2 They can sing.
3 They can swim.
4 We can dance.
5 We can't dance.
6 He can't swim.
7 They can't sing.
8 He can't ride a bike.

 A
 E
 B
 F
 C
 G
 D
 H

2 ★★☆ **Match the questions and answers.**

0 Can you and Morag sing?   e
1 Can you speak Italian?   ☐
2 Can Davide play the violin?   ☐
3 Can Helen cook?   ☐
4 Can a Ferrari go fast?   ☐
5 Can Karim and Jake ride a bike?   ☐

a No, he can't.
b Yes, they can.
c Yes, I can.
d Yes, it can.
e No, we can't.
f Yes, she can.

3 ★★★ **Write sentences with *can* and *can't*.**

0 I / ride a bike (✓) / roller-skate (✗)
   I can ride a bike, but I can't roller-skate.

1 I / sing (✓) / dance (✗)
   _____

2 my little sister / talk (✗) / walk (✓)
   _____

3 they / speak Spanish (✓) / speak Turkish (✗)
   _____

4 my brother / drive (✗) / cook (✓)
   _____

5 we / jump high (✗) / run fast (✓)
   _____

6 my grandmother / play the piano (✗) /
   play the guitar (✓)
   _____

7 birds / sing (✓) / talk (✗)
   _____

PRONUNCIATION
Long vowel sound /ɔː/   **Go to page 120.**

4 ★★★ **Look at the pictures and write questions with *can*. Then answer them so they are true for you.**

0

Can you drive?
No, I can't.

1

_____
_____

2

_____
_____

3

_____
_____

4

_____
_____

5 ★★★ **Complete the sentences with your own ideas.**

1 I can't _____ ,
  but I can _____ .
2 My best friend can _____ ,
  but he/she can't _____ .
3 My teacher can't _____ ,
  but he/she can _____ .
4 Babies can _____ ,
  but they can't _____ .
5 My mum can _____ ,
  but she can't _____ .
6 My dad can't _____ ,
  but he can _____ .
7 The cat can _____ ,
  but it can't _____ .

Prepositions of time

 SB p.71

6 ★☆☆ **Circle the correct options.**

0 I leave home *at* / *in* / *on* 7 am to go to school.
1 Julieta's birthday is *at* / *in* / *on* May.
2 The match starts *at* / *in* / *on* 8 pm.
3 It's very hot *at* / *in* / *on* summer.
4 I don't go to school *at* / *in* / *on* Sundays.
5 There's a holiday *at* / *in* / *on* 7th April this year.
6 We play volleyball *at* / *in* / *on* Friday afternoons.
7 The first day of school is *at* / *in* / *on* autumn.

7 ★★☆ **Complete the sentences with *at*, *in* or *on*.**

0 The party is on Saturday ____*at*____ 7 pm.
1 School starts _____ 8 am and it finishes _____ 3 pm.
2 It's not very cold _____ spring.
3 My school holidays start _____ June and finish _____ September.
4 My birthday is _____ 1st April. It's _____ spring. This year it's _____ a Monday.

8 ★★☆ **Write the words in the correct columns.**

> Friday | May | midday | midnight
> September | seven o'clock
> the evening | the morning | Tuesday
> 3.30 pm | 22nd May | 7th July

in	on	at
May		

GET IT RIGHT!

Prepositions of time

We use *on* for days of the week and dates.

✓ I go swimming on Saturday.
✗ I go swimming in Saturday.
✓ Her birthday is on 1st May.
✗ Her birthday is in 1st May.

We use *at* for clock times.

✓ My dance lesson is at five o'clock.
✗ My dance lesson is on five o'clock.

We use *in* for months and seasons.

✓ Is your birthday in November?
✗ Is your birthday at November?
✓ We often go to the beach in summer.
✗ We often go to the beach at summer.

Complete the sentences with *at*, *in* or *on*.

0 I will be there ____*on*____ Sunday evening.
1 He wants to have a party _____ 7th July.
2 I can come _____ Monday or Friday.
3 My school exams are _____ June.
4 Can you meet me _____ half past ten?
5 The trees are pretty _____ autumn.
6 It starts _____ quarter to eight.

VOCABULARY
Sport

1 ★★★ **Look at the pictures and write sentences.**

0 Carlo	1 Lewis
2 Megan	3 Adam
4 Liz	5 Ethan
6 Amelia	7 Marta

0 _____Carlo skis._____   4 _____
1 _____   5 _____
2 _____   6 _____
3 _____   7 _____

Telling the time

→ SB p.69

2 ★★☆ **Write the times under the clocks.**

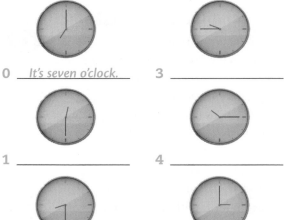

0 _It's seven o'clock._   3 _____

1 _____   4 _____

2 _____   5 _____

Months and seasons

→ SB p.71

3 ★★☆ **Complete the months and seasons with the missing consonants.**

Months
1 O _ _ o _ e _   9 _ e _ _ e _ _ e _
2 _ u _ e   10 _ o _ e _ _ e _
3 A _ _ i _   11 _ e _ _ u a _ _
4 _ e _ e _ _ e _   12 _ a _ _ _
5 _ a _   **Seasons**
6 _ u _ _   13 _ u _ _ e _
7 _ a _ u a _ _   14 a u _ u _ _
8 A u _ u _ _   15 _ _ _ i _ _
                     16 _ i _ _ e _

4 ★★★ **Choose four months. Say what season they are in and what you do in each month.**

0 _August is in summer. I go on holiday with my_
family in August.

1 _____
_____
_____

2 _____
_____

3 _____
_____

4 _____
_____
_____

Ordinal numbers

→ SB p.71

5 ★☆☆ **Complete the table.**

1st	first	9th	
	second	10th	
3rd			eleventh
4th		12th	
	fifth		thirteenth
6th		20th	
7th		30th	
8th			thirty-first

6 ★★☆ **Write the ordinal numbers.**

0 14th _____fourteenth_____
1 21st _____
2 27th _____
3 22nd _____
4 28th _____
5 15th _____
6 16th _____
7 23rd _____
8 29th _____
9 24th _____
10 17th _____
11 18th _____
12 19th _____
13 26th _____
14 25th _____

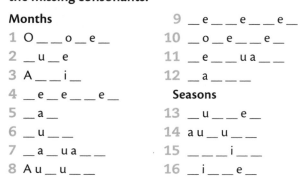

REFERENCE

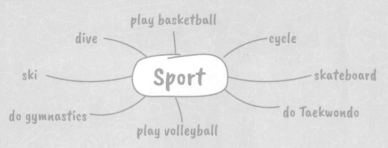

Sport — play basketball, dive, cycle, ski, skateboard, do gymnastics, do Taekwondo, play volleyball

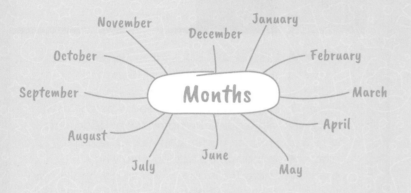

Months — November, December, January, October, February, September, March, August, April, July, June, May

Ordinal numbers

1st – first	5th – fifth	9th – ninth	13th – thirteenth
2nd – second	6th – sixth	10th – tenth	20th – twentieth
3rd – third	7th – seventh	11th – eleventh	30th – thirtieth
4th – fourth	8th – eighth	12th – twelfth	31st – thirty-first

Telling the time

1 It's three o'clock.

2 It's half past eight.

3 It's quarter past ten.

4 It's quarter to one.

Seasons — winter, spring, autumn, summer

VOCABULARY *EXTRA*

1 Match the objects in the pictures with the sports from the list.

badminton | frisbee | karate | netball | running | table football

1 _____ 2 _____ 3 _____ 4 _____ 5 _____ 6 _____

2 Complete the sentences with the correct sport from Exercise 1.

1 We often play _____ in the café near my house.

2 Girls at my school play _____ . It's a bit like basketball.

3 To go _____ , all you need is a pair of trainers.

4 When you play _____ , you use a racket, but not a ball.

5 I do _____ , a Japanese martial art.

6 Lots of people play _____ in the park.

SPORT FOR ALL

The Paralympic Games are a big sporting event for athletes with disabilities. The Games show the world all the amazing things that these athletes can do. They take place every two years: after the Summer Olympics, and after the Winter Olympics. Here are two incredible Paralympians.

This is ³_____ .
He's from ⁴_____ .

Jessica Long is American. Jessica has no legs below the knee, but she's a fantastic swimmer. She can swim really fast, using only her arms and body. She's a very successful Paralympian. She has got lots of gold medals from several different Paralympic Games! Jessica loves sport, and also plays basketball and goes ice-skating, cycling and rock-climbing. Another interesting fact about Jessica is the date of her birthday. It's 29th February – this happens only every four years!

Jaryd Clifford is Australian. He can't see very well, but he can run really fast. He can run 1,500 metres in 3 minutes 47 seconds – in the top ten for *all* athletes in Australia! Because he can't see, Jaryd runs with a guide. His name is Tim Logan, and he's a good runner, too. Tim can see, so he helps Jaryd stay on the track, and tells Jaryd where the other runners are. Tim is also Jaryd's friend, and knows him well, so they are a good team. Jaryd is young, but he's already very successful. He's got lots of medals, including a gold one, and a world record. He wants to get even better in the future!

This is ¹_____ .
She's from ²_____ .

READING

1 **Read the text and complete the sentences under the pictures.**

2 **Read the text again and answer the questions.**
   1 When do the Paralympics happen? _____
   2 How does Jessica swim? _____
   3 Has Jessica got medals from more than one Paralympics? _____
   4 What is different about Jessica's birthday? _____
   _____
   5 What can't Jaryd Clifford do? _____
   6 How does he stay on the track? _____
   7 Why are Jaryd and Tim a good team? _____
   _____

3 **CRITICAL THINKING Read the information about the athletes. Is each sentence about Jessica (JL) or Jaryd (JC) ?**
   1 _____ can win races with athletes who haven't got a disability.
   2 _____ spends a lot of time doing different sports.
   3 _____ has got a lot of gold medals over many years.
   4 A good friend helps _____ to be an amazing athlete.
   5 _____ doesn't have a birthday every year.
   6 _____ has got a world record.

An amazing person

1 INPUT **Read the text. What sport is mentioned?**

MY AMAZING GRANDMA

My grandma Ana is an amazing person. We live in the same city, Madrid, so I see her a lot. She's 72 years old and she still swims every day. She's in a team at a swimming club and does races most weekends. She swims in special races for people over 65. She always wins. She's really fast. She can swim 400 metres in five minutes. She loves swimming. It makes her feel young. I like her because she's a great swimmer, she's fun, and she makes lovely cakes!

2 ANALYSE **Imagine you're the writer of the text and answer the questions.**

0 Who is she?
My grandma Ana.

1 Where does she live?
_____

2 What does she do?
_____

3 What sort of amazing things can she do?
_____

4 Why do you like her?
_____

3 PLAN **Make notes about an amazing person you know.**

1 Who is he/she?
_____

2 Where does he/she live?
_____

3 How old is he/she?
_____

4 What sort of amazing things can he/she do?
_____

5 Why do you like him/her?
_____

 WRITING TIP: Third person 's' for *he*, *she* and *it*

In English it's easy to forget the 's' at the end of verbs in the third person singular!

She swims every day.
She does races.
It makes her feel young.

4 PRODUCE **Use your answers to the questions in Exercise 3 to write a short text about your person. Write about 60 words.**

_____
_____
_____
_____
_____
_____
_____
_____
_____
_____

🎧 LISTENING

1 🔊 7.03 **Listen and match the conversations with the pictures. Write 1–3 in the boxes.**

A ☐

B ☐

C ☐

2 🔊 7.03 **Listen again and draw the times on the clocks.**

Conversation 1:
What time do they play tennis?

Conversation 2:
What time is the film they choose?

Conversation 3:
What time do they meet?

3 🔊 7.03 **Listen again and complete each sentence with one word.**

0 Louise feels a bit _____*bored*_____ .

1 Louise is _____ until 1 pm.

2 Rosie wants to go to the cinema in the
_____ .

3 The first film is at _____ past six.

4 Lucy wants to go _____ with Dan.

5 Lucy finishes _____ at five.

DIALOGUE

4 **Put the conversation in order.**

☐ **Ben** We can't. We haven't got a frisbee.

☐ **Ben** Videos! That's why I'm bored. I'm tired of watching videos.

☐ **Ben** We can't. She's on holiday.

☐ 1 **Ben** I'm bored. What can we do?

☐ **Selma** Is she? So how about some more videos?

☐ **Selma** Why don't we play frisbee?

☐ **Selma** No frisbee? OK, let's go to Eva's house.

PHRASES FOR FLUENCY → SB p.72

5 **Match the questions with the answers.**

0 Are these your things? ☐ c

1 Oh, no, look at the rain. ☐

2 Where's Cape Town? ☐

3 Look, there goes the bus. <u>Now what</u>? ☐

a <u>It's no big deal</u>. I've got an umbrella.

b <u>I'm sure</u> it's in South Africa.

c No, I think that's Dean's <u>stuff</u>.

d Don't worry. There's another one in 15 minutes.

6 **Complete the dialogue with the words and phrases that are underlined in Exercise 5.**

Mum Come on, Owen. It's time for school.

Owen I'm ready, Mum.

Mum Have you got your swimming
0 _____*stuff*_____ ?

Owen I haven't got a swimming lesson today.

Mum **1**_____ you have, Owen.
It's Thursday.

Owen Thursday! Oh, no. I have got a swimming lesson!
But my towel's wet. **2**_____ ?

Mum **3**_____ . You can take
another towel.

Owen Thanks, Mum. You're the best!

SUM IT UP

1 **Read and write the names of the sports.**

Welcome to a day of **sport** on B C B TV.

We've got a great programme of sporting action for you this Saturday.

We've got live _____ 0 ___football___ from Anfield, where Liverpool play Manchester City in the big game.

We've got _____ 1 _____ with ALL the action from the NBA.

There's _____ 2 _____ action from last night's match between Brazil and China.

There's live _____ 3 _____ from the World Championships in Copenhagen.

And we've got _____ 4 _____ from the Alpine World Cup, this weekend in Croatia.

There's something for everyone!

2 **Read the clues and complete the TV sports programmes.**

Start time	Finish time	Sports programme
1 pm	1.30 pm	
pm	pm	
pm	pm	
pm	pm	
pm	pm	

1 The afternoon of sport starts at 1 pm.
2 Gymnastics is the fourth programme.
3 The skiing is on for half an hour.
4 Football is after volleyball.
5 Basketball starts six hours after skiing finishes.
6 The football starts at 3 pm.

7 Gymnastics is on for two and a half hours.
8 Volleyball is on for an hour and a half.
9 There are eight hours of sport.
10 Skiing is the first sport.
11 The last programme is 90 minutes long.

3 **Put the words in the list into four categories. There are three words in each category. Name the categories.**

August | cycling | fifth | first | June | May | snowboarding | spring | summer | Taekwondo | third | winter

1 MONTHS	2	3	4
August			

8 FEEL THE RHYTHM

Grammar rap!
▶ 23

G GRAMMAR
Present continuous
→ SB p.76

1 ⭐☆☆ (Circle) the correct options.

0 She isn't here. She('s)/ 're skateboarding in the park.
1 What *is / are* you doing?
2 Sorry, I can't talk now. I *'m / is* watching a film.
3 All my friends are here. We *'s / 're* having a great time!
4 My brother's in his room. He *'s / 're* playing computer games.
5 My mum and dad *is / are* shopping at the supermarket.
6 I think they're happy. They *'s / 're* smiling a lot!
7 Look! There's Zack. Where *'s / 're* he going?

2 ⭐☆☆ Write the *-ing* form of these verbs.

0 shop _____*shopping*_____
1 play _____
2 give _____
3 sit _____
4 dance _____
5 smile _____
6 run _____
7 walk _____
8 read _____
9 take _____
10 try _____
11 stop _____
12 write _____
13 draw _____

3 ⭐⭐☆ Complete the sentences with the present continuous form of the verbs in brackets.

0 Go away, Li. I ___*'m not talking*___ to you! (not talk)
1 Let's go for a walk. It _____ . (not rain)
2 _____ you _____ the party? (enjoy)
3 _____ your brother _____ a good time at university? (have)
4 What _____ you _____ , Joaquim? (do)
5 The TV is on, but they _____ it. (not watch)
6 Ivy! You _____ to me! (not listen)
7 What _____ the cat _____ ? (eat)
8 They _____ well today. (not play)

4 ⭐⭐☆ Lily is telling Juan about a new quiz show on TV. Complete the conversation with the present continuous form of the verbs in brackets.

Lily Hey Juan, how are you? Are you free this evening?

Juan Hmm, I'm not sure. Why?

Lily Well, there's a great new quiz show on TV. There are two teams. When it starts, one player in a team 0_____*is watching*_____ (watch) a video on a tablet. Of course, the other players can't see what 1_____ (happen) on the screen.

Juan So?

Lily Well, the player with the tablet says things like 'A boy 2_____ (run). He 3_____ (wear) shorts. He 4_____ (hold) a ball.' After each sentence, the other players guess what 5_____ (happen) in the video.

Juan And then what?

Lily The players can ask ten questions.

Juan Like 'What 6_____ they _____ (do) in the video?'

Lily No, of course not. They can only ask questions like '7_____ the boy _____ (play) with friends?' or '8_____ they _____ (go) to school?' or '9_____ they _____ (watch) a game of football?'

Juan And then?

Lily Sometimes the player watching the video says what 10_____ (not happen) in the video. Things like 'The boy 11_____ (not sitting) on the floor' or 'The people 12_____ (not play) music.' And the other player gets a point if they can say what's happening in the video.

Juan Hmm. I don't like watching quiz shows. I like watching films.

Lily Oh. Well, please watch tonight. There's a surprise for you!

Juan A surprise? For me? Now I want to watch it!

72

5 ★★★ **Complete this extract from the quiz show with the correct form of the verbs in the list.**

> hit | hold | kick | not go | not smile
> not throw | play (x3) | stand | ~~wear~~

Host Right! Let's play! Lily, you have the tablet, so your team starts.

Lily Well, I can see 12 girls here. They
0 ___'re wearing___ shorts and T-shirts.

Simon 1 _____ they _____ a game?

Lily Yes, they are. They 2 _____ with a ball.

Ibra 3 _____ they _____ the ball with their feet?

Lily No, they aren't. And they 4 _____ the ball. One girl 5 _____ the ball in her hand. She 6 _____ behind a line on the floor.

Zehra 7 _____ she _____ the ball with her hand?

Lily Yes, she is. But the ball 8 _____ into the net. That's not good. She isn't happy. She 9 _____ .

Ibra I know! 10 _____ they _____ volleyball?

Lily Yes, they are!

Host Well done! That's one point to you.

6 ★★★ **What do you think your family and friends are doing now? Look at the example and write similar sentences about them.**

0 *I think my sister is reading a magazine now.*
1 _____
2 _____
3 _____
4 _____
5 _____

like / don't like + -ing   → SB p.78

7 ★★☆ **Write sentences with the correct form of the verbs.**

0 I / like / read / long books
I like reading long books.

1 my sister / not like / do / gymnastics
_____

2 my parents / hate / watch / romantic films
_____

3 my best friend / like / listen to / classical music
_____

4 I / not like / go to / buy clothes
_____

5 I / love / read / in bed
_____

8 ★★☆ **Complete the text. Use** *love* (:) :))**,** *like* (:))**,** *don't/doesn't like* (:( )**,** *hate* (:(:( ) **and the correct form of the verbs.**

> My family are a bit strange – they like or don't like all kinds of different things. My sister 0 *doesn't like cooking* (:(cook) but she 1 _____ (:) :) clean) her room. My father 2 _____ (:(:(go) for walks, but he 3 _____ (:) do) exercise classes at the gym. My mother 4 _____ (:) read) books, but she 5 _____ (:(:(look) at magazines. My parents 6 _____ (:) :) travel) to other countries, but they 7 _____ (:(speak) other languages. And me? Well, I just 8 _____ (:) :) be) with my strange family!

9 ★★☆ **Complete the sentences so they are true for you.**

0 I love ___*singing in the shower*___ and ___*dancing in my bedroom*___ .

1 I love _____ and _____ .

2 I like _____ and _____ .

3 I don't like _____ and _____ .

4 I hate _____ and _____ .

GET IT RIGHT!

Present continuous

We use subject + *am/is/are* + *-ing* form of the main verb.

✓ *We are watching a video.*
✗ *We watching a video.*
✓ *I am eating a sandwich.*
✗ *I am eat a sandwich.*

Complete the sentences with the correct present continuous form of the verbs in brackets.

0 She ___*is taking*___ (take) some photos of her food.

1 We _____ (do) the shopping at the moment.

2 _____ (you / listen) to rap music?

3 He _____ (wear) a red shirt and black trousers.

4 They _____ (walk) to the sports centre.

5 Who _____ (play) computer games?

6 He _____ (not eat) a sandwich, he's eating cake!

VOCABULARY
Present continuous verbs

→ SB p.76

1 ★☆☆ **Look at the picture above and complete the sentences with the correct form of the verbs from the list.**

cheer | dance | leave | read | ~~run~~ | sing
sit | smile | stand | take | talk | wear

0 Pierre is __running__ .
1 Elena is _____ .
2 Charlie is _____ .
3 Lucy is _____ on a bench.
4 Lucas and Kerry are _____ .
5 Callum is _____ a hat.
6 Helena is _____ .
7 Rob is _____ .
8 Claire is _____ on her phone.
9 Matt is _____ a photo.
10 Fiona is _____ .
11 Jen and Pablo are _____ the park.

2 ★★☆ **Complete each sentence with a verb from Exercise 1. Use the correct form of the verbs.**

0 I'm __reading__ a really good book. It's very interesting!
1 My dad's crazy. He wants to _____ a marathon.
2 Let's _____ a song.
3 This train _____ at 10.45, and arrives in Barcelona at 12.40.
4 Look at Mike! He's _____ green trousers and a purple jumper!
5 Can you _____ a photo of us, please?
6 I love _____ on the phone with my friends.
7 This is my favourite chair. I love _____ here.

Clothes

→ SB p.79

3 ★★☆ **Find 11 more clothes items in the word search.**

T	R	O	U	D	E	D	J	A	N	S	T
A	S	H	I	R	T	R	A	S	E	H	P
S	A	T	H	L	O	E	W	K	S	I	O
T	R	E	A	I	N	S	X	C	R	R	R
S	N	A	E	J	O	S	H	O	E	S	E
H	T	L	O	T	S	A	U	S	S	W	P
E	R	B	K	R	H	B	N	Y	U	E	M
R	I	R	W	E	O	U	K	J	O	A	U
L	H	A	D	I	R	Y	L	U	R	F	J
P	S	C	O	A	T	T	R	N	T	E	A
J	T	R	I	K	S	G	E	S	A	R	M
U	M	B	E	T	R	A	I	N	E	R	S

4 ★★☆ **Circle the odd one out in each list.**

0 (jeans) — jumper — shirt
1 socks — trainers — coat
2 shorts — T-shirt — trousers
3 dress — skirt — shoes
4 jumper — T-shirt — coat

5 ★★★ **Write answers to the questions so they are true for you.**

1 What clothes do you love wearing at the weekend?
_____

2 What clothes do you never buy?
_____

3 Of all the people you know, who wears really nice clothes? What do they wear?
_____

PRONUNCIATION
Intonation – listing items Go to page 120.

REFERENCE
Verbs

base form	-ing form
cheer	cheering
dance	dancing
leave	leaving
read	reading
run	running
sing	singing
sit	sitting
smile	smiling
stand	standing
take	taking
talk	talking
wear	wearing

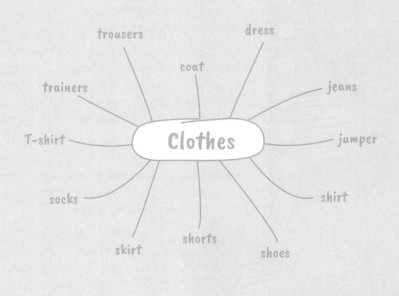

Clothes: trousers, coat, dress, trainers, jeans, T-shirt, jumper, socks, shirt, skirt, shorts, shoes

VOCABULARY *EXTRA*

1 **Label the picture with the words from the list of clothes.**

handbag | necklace | raincoat | suit | tie | umbrella

2 **Complete the sentences with words from the list in Exercise 1.**

1 Our school uniform has black trousers, a white shirt and a red _____ .

2 It's raining! You need to wear your _____ and take an _____ .

3 Gio's dad doesn't want to wear a _____ every day to work. He likes jeans and T-shirts!

4 'That's a beautiful _____ .'
'It's a birthday present for my sister. It's gold.'

5 'Oh no! I can't find my _____ . My new phone's in it!'
'Don't worry, Mum. It's on the sofa.'

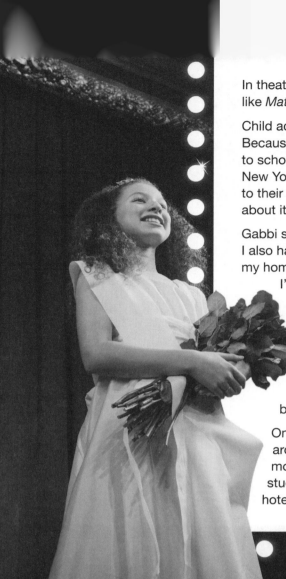

In theatres around the world, musicals are very popular. And some shows, like *Matilda* and *Harry Potter*, have child actors. So what is their life like?

Child actors need to study, but this doesn't mean they go to school. Because they perform at night, often until late, it's difficult for them to go to school every day. So they often study at home. Many child actors in New York study at a special online school. They can add virtual lessons to their personal routine. Let's ask some child actors in a New York show about it!

Gabbi says, 'I watch the lessons, and I can talk to the teachers online. I also have a "learning coach" – my mom! She helps me study and do my homework, and we choose the lessons together. At the moment, I'm studying six subjects.'

'It's not easy,' says Daya. 'There is a show most afternoons and one every night, so it's difficult to do all the work the teachers give us and get good marks. I am not in every show though (two other girls play the same part as me), and that way we all have time for schoolwork and other things – I'm also taking dancing and singing lessons. The other girls aren't doing that, but they love playing video games and reading.'

Online learning is also good because child actors sometimes move around. Daya explains, 'My play isn't showing in New York at the moment. We're touring the US and Canada with the show, and we're studying for school exams. We stay in each town for a week, in a hotel. It's a great life! We love it!'

📖 READING

1 **Read the article about child actors. Do they work all the time? What else do they do?**

2 **Read the article again and mark the sentences T (true) or F (false). Correct the false statements.**

0 Musicals aren't popular around the world.   [F]
They are very popular.

1 Child actors all have to continue their education.   ☐
_____

2 Theatre shows never finish late.   ☐
_____

3 All New York child actors study online.   ☐
_____

4 They talk to the teachers by mobile phone.   ☐
_____

5 When you're in a play, there are often two shows a day.   ☐
_____

6 Three different children sometimes play the same part.   ☐
_____

7 Daya is performing in New York now.   ☐
_____

3 CRITICAL THINKING **Imagine you are a child actor in the theatre. What do you like about it? What don't you like about it? Why? Use ideas from this list or your own ideas. Write sentences.**

- getting up early / going to bed late
- organising your day
- schoolwork and homework
- having fun with friends

_____
_____
_____
_____
_____
_____
_____
_____
_____
_____

DEVELOPING *Writing*

Describing a scene

1  **Read Dalia's email. Why is everyone busy?**

⭐ **Elif**
Dalia@thinkmail.com

Hi Elif,

It's Sunday morning. The sun is shining.
I'm sitting in my room. I love sitting here.
It's usually quiet and I like watching the birds
in the garden. But the garden is busy today.
My parents are having a summer party to
celebrate being married for 25 years!!

There's a big tent in the garden. We're
having lunch in the tent. My parents are
moving tables and chairs. They're laughing
and making lots of noise. There are some
people walking into the kitchen. They are
carrying big boxes of food and drink for
the party. Uh oh! Now my dad's calling me.
He's choosing the party music. His favourite
songs are really old, so he wants me to
help him!

What are you doing today?

Dalia

2 **ANALYSE** **Match the parts of the phrases. Then read the email again and check your answers.**

0	watching	a	big boxes
1	choosing	b	the birds
2	having	c	party music
3	moving	d	tables and chairs
4	carrying	e	a party

3 **PLAN** **Imagine it's Sunday morning. Use the ideas below and make notes.**

a Choose a place:
  - the shopping centre   • your house
  - the beach   • another place

b What are you doing? What's happening near you?
  Who can you see and what are they doing? Use these
  verbs to help you.

  buy | have | listen | play | read | sit | watch

  _____
  _____
  _____
  _____
  _____

c Something happens – it changes things. What happens?

  _____
  _____
  _____
  _____
  _____

4 **PRODUCE** **Use your notes to write an email to a friend about your Sunday morning. Use the email in Exercise 1 to help you. Write about 60 words.**

 **WRITING TIP: Starting an email**

Start with *Hi* + your friend's name and a comma (,).
Then start the email on the next line.

LISTENING

1 🔊 8.02 **Listen to a boy phoning his sister and choose the correct answer.**

1 Right now, he is in the hotel *bedroom / reception*.

2 After the call, he is going to *Buckingham Palace / the theatre*.

2 🔊 8.02 **Listen again and complete the sentences with one word.**

0 The boy's sister's name is ___Petra___ .

1 He's on a class trip to _____ .

2 From his hotel room he can see some girls riding _____ .

3 One couple he can see are wearing very smart _____ .

4 His sister thinks the couple are going to the _____ .

5 She forgets that Ricky is going see *The Lion King* _____ .

6 Ricky is wearing smart _____ and his best blue _____ .

7 Petra wants Ricky to ring her again _____ .

DIALOGUE

3 🔊 8.03 **Listen to Stefan interviewing Alicia for a school project. How many questions does he ask her?**

_____

4 🔊 8.03 **Listen again and complete the conversation.**

Stefan Hi, Alicia! I'd like to ask you some questions. Is that okay?

Alicia Yeah, sure. What about?

Stefan What do you like doing in the evenings?

Alicia You mean, after school? Well, I like ⁰ *chatting to friends online* and I love ¹_____ .

Stefan And what about the weekends?

Alicia On Saturday, I help clean the house. I like ²_____ , but I hate ³_____ the dishes. And on Sunday, I like ⁴_____ with my friends in the park or ⁵_____ to the cinema.

Stefan Thanks, Alicia. Now I can finish my school project.

Alicia Good thing! It's only ten minutes until class!

5 **Now Stefan is interviewing his grandpa. Put Grandpa's answers in the correct order.**

Stefan Grandpa, can I ask you some questions, please?

Grandpa Yes, of course. What do you want to know?

Stefan Well, what do you like doing in the evenings?

Grandpa ⁰ films / I / watching / love
I love watching films.

Stefan And what about the weekends?

Grandpa ¹ On / I / at / the / football club / Saturdays / like / friends / meeting / my

_____

² I / On / visit / usually / house / Sundays / your

_____

³ family / seeing / I / my / love

_____

⁴ I / don't / your music / listening / like / to / But / always

_____

Stefan Thanks a lot, Grandpa.

6 **Imagine that Stefan is interviewing you. Complete the answers to his questions so they are true for you.**

Stefan What do you like doing in the evenings?

You I like _____ and I love _____ .

Stefan What about the weekend?

You On Saturday, I like _____ and on Sunday, I like _____ .

Stefan What do you hate doing?

You I hate _____ .

Stefan And what are you doing now?

You I'm _____ .

Train to TH!NK

Memorising

7 🔊 8.02 **Listen to Ricky and Petra again. Read the questions (1–5) that Petra asks Ricky. Can you remember Ricky's answers to the questions? Write them down.**

1 How's your class trip going?
_____ !

2 What's your room like?
_____ !

3 What are you doing now?
_____ .

4 What are you doing tonight?
Petra, _____ , remember?

5 Are you wearing a suit, ha ha?
What _____ ?
_____ !

8 🔊 8.02 **Listen one more time and check your answers.**

EXAM SKILLS: READING
Answering multiple-choice questions

1   **Read Monika's email to her friend Paulo and answer the questions.**

    1 Where is Monika? _____

    2 What does she want to see there? _____

  Paulo
Monika@thinkmail.com

Hi Paulo,

How are you? I'm on holiday – well, you know that, right? – and I'm having a great time here in Granada. We're staying in a nice hotel near the city centre. It's small, but it's cheap and very comfortable, and we like it. The people who work here speak good English. That's great, because my family doesn't speak Spanish! Well, I know a few words now – *gracias* and *por favor*, that kind of thing! I can say *Tengo hambre*, too. That means 'I'm hungry', and you know me, I'm always hungry!

Granada is a cool place. The famous Alhambra palace is here. It's very beautiful. And it's a great place for Flamenco, too. I love Flamenco dancing and I want to see some here. Oh, just a minute – my mum says that Dad is on his tablet and he's getting tickets for a Flamenco show tonight here in the city! Great!

Hope you're well. Please write soon, OK?

Monika

2   **Read the email again. Choose the correct answers (A, B or C).**

    0 Monika's family are staying in a _____ hotel.

      A big   Ⓑ comfortable   **C** expensive

    1 The people at the hotel _____ English.

      A like   **B** don't understand   **C** understand

    2 Monika knows _____ words in Spanish.

      A some   **B** a lot of   **C** no

    3 In Granada there is a famous _____ .

      A palace   **B** dance clubs   **C** cool place

    4 Monika's _____ has a tablet.

      A father   **B** mother   **C** Flamenco

    5 Monika's father _____ a Flamenco show.

      A isn't getting tickets for   **B** is buying tickets for   **C** is reading a book about

📖 READING TIP

When the questions about a text are multiple choice, it means you have to choose the one correct answer from three or four possibilities.

- Look for items that are grammatically wrong. For example, in the following question, A is wrong because we can't have 'a' before a vowel, and C is wrong because we can't use 'some' before a singular noun.

   He's eating _____ apple.

   A a   **B** an   **C** some

- Look for words that have similar meanings. For example, in Question 5 of Exercise 2, 'buying' and 'getting' have the same meaning.

- You must check all three (or four) options before you decide which one is correct.

CONSOLIDATION

🎧 LISTENING

1 🔊 8.04 **Listen to Daniela and circle the correct answers (A, B or C).**

1 Daniela's birthday is …
  A 20th October.
  B 21st October.
  C 1st October.

2 Daniela's camera is a present from …
  A her grandparents.
  B her brother.
  C her mother and father.

3 Daniela's favourite season is …
  A winter.
  B autumn.
  C summer.

2 🔊 8.04 **Listen again and complete the words.**

1 Daniela is f_____ .
2 She thinks Ipswich isn't e_____ .
3 Daniela is having d_____ lessons.
4 Daniela's got special s_____ for dancing.
5 Daniela's friends like s_____ .
6 Daniela likes w_____ on cold days.

 GRAMMAR

3 **Circle the correct options.**

Bella Hi, Kurt. What ¹*are / is* you doing?

Kurt Oh, hi, Bella. ²*I wait / I'm waiting* for my dad. And you?

Bella I'm doing some shopping. I'm not ³*buying / buy* much – just some stuff for school. Hey, you've got new headphones. They look great!

Kurt Yeah, thanks! ⁴*I'm listening / I listen* to a lot of music. Waiting is boring! I ⁵*can't / don't can* wait without music!

Bella What ⁶*do you listen / are you listening* to right now?

Kurt It's some violin music. I really like ⁷*listen / listening* to violin music.

Bella ⁸*Can you / Do you can* play the violin, Kurt?

Kurt No, I ⁹*can't / can*. But I often ¹⁰*listen / am listening* to it!

---

4 **Charlie is showing Eva a video on his phone. Put the words in order to make sentences.**

0 is / Liam / brother / This / my
  This is my brother Liam.

1 an old people's home / He's / arriving at
  _____

2 meeting / He / his friends / is
  _____

3 Liam's / today / the guitar / his friends / playing /with
  _____

4 are / at the old people's home / They / giving / a concert
  _____

5 a chair / is / on / Liam / sitting
  _____

6 next to / is / him / My friend Amanda / standing
  _____

7 Beatles / singing / songs / They're / old
  _____

8 are / The / with / them / old people / singing
  _____

🔤 VOCABULARY

5 **Put the words from the list into three groups. Give each group a title. Then write one more word in each group.**

> August | dress | February | golf | gymnastics | jeans
> jumper | June | May | surfing | tennis | trainers

1 months	2	3

6 **Complete the sentences with the words from the list. There are two extra words.**

> cheer | dance | dancing | second
> summer | talk | two | watching

1 My birthday is the _____ of March.
2 I've got a problem with my foot, so I can't _____ tonight.
3 Every week, I _____ to my grandparents in Spain on the phone.
4 I like listening to music, but I don't like _____ to it!
5 We always _____ when our team wins.
6 It's great here in the _____ when the weather is hot.

DIALOGUE

7 🔊 8.05 **Put the conversations in order. Then listen and check.**

Conversation 1

☐ **Ecrin** Great idea! I love cooking. Let's check we've got everything we need.

☐ **Ecrin** No, it's five o'clock. The shops close at half past five.

☐ **Ecrin** I'm really bored.

☐ **Seda** Me, too. Why don't we go into town? We can go shopping.

☐ **Seda** Oh yes! OK, how about making a cake?

Conversation 2

☐ **Rico** OK, it's no big deal. We can stay here in my house. I've got a good book to read.

☐ **Rico** Hey, how about going for a walk?

☐ **Rico** Yes, I'm sure I can find one for you.

☐ **Zara** Great idea! I love reading. Have you got a book for me, too?

☐ **Zara** No thanks! It's cold outside. And I don't like walking very much.

📖 READING

8 **Read the phone conversation. Then complete the sentences with the correct information.**

Niall Hey Ella, what are you doing?

Ella I'm talking to you on the phone, ha ha!

Niall Yes, very funny. But seriously – what are you doing?

Ella Nothing really. I'm just sitting in my room. Why?

Niall How about coming to the park? That's where I am now!

Ella The park? Why? What's happening in the park?

Niall There's a race today. It's a ten-kilometre run. My parents are running in it.

Ella Are they crazy? It's winter! It's cold and it's raining.

Niall It isn't raining very much. And I'm wearing a warm coat and shoes. So, I'm OK.

Ella Well, no thanks. I like being warm, not cold.

Niall OK, it's no big deal. Oh, and Mark Watson's running in the race. I can see him, too.

Ella Really? Mark Watson from our school?

Niall Yes, him. And at the moment, he's first – he's winning!

Ella Right, I'm putting my coat on and I'm leaving the house now.

Niall Really?

Ella Yes – Mark Watson's there, so I want to be there, too!

Niall Oh, OK. See you soon then!

1 Ella is in _____ .

2 Niall is in _____ .

3 There's a _____-kilometre race today.

4 Niall's _____ and _____ are running in the race.

5 Niall _____ cold because he's _____ a warm coat.

6 Ella doesn't like _____ .

7 Mark Watson is a boy from their _____ .

8 Mark is _____ the race.

9 Ella is _____ the house because she wants to _____ .

✏️ WRITING

9 **Write a short dialogue between two friends. Write about 60 words. Use these ideas to help you.**

- one friend is bored
- the other friend suggests something to do
- the first friend doesn't like the idea very much
- the second friend suggests another thing to do (go for a walk, go to the cinema, play video games, etc.)

9 WHO'S HUNGRY?

Grammar rap!

▶ 26

 GRAMMAR

must / mustn't   → SB p.86

1 ★☆☆ **Complete the sentences with *must* or *mustn't*.**

My very healthy mum says:

0 I __mustn't__ drink too much cola.
1 I _____ eat more vegetables.
2 I _____ eat sweets or chocolate before meals.
3 I _____ go to bed late.
4 I _____ do sports after school.
5 I _____ drink more water.

2 ★☆☆ **the correct options.**

0 A Dad, have we got any fruit?
   B No, we haven't. I (must) / mustn't buy some.
1 A Do you want to come to my house after school?
   B I can't. I've got a clarinet lesson tomorrow so I *must / mustn't* practise tonight.
2 A What day is it today?
   B It's Wednesday. We've got PE this morning. You *must / mustn't* forget your PE clothes.
3 A What a cute hamster! Can we take it home?
   B OK, but you *must / mustn't* look after it.
4 A I'm not ready yet.
   B Hurry up then. We *must / mustn't* miss the train.
5 A I'm ready, Mum.
   B Good. The film starts in an hour and we *must / mustn't* be late.
6 A Hey Dad, can I have one of these apples?
   B Yes, but you *must / mustn't* wash it before you eat it.

3 ★★★ **Complete the sentences with *must* (✓) or *mustn't* (✗) and a verb from the list.**

be | buy | eat | finish | forget
give | remember | wash | ~~write~~

0 Ellie ___must write___ an email to her friend Miray in Istanbul. (✓)
1 Marcus _____ home late today. (✗)
2 Helena _____ to take her tablet to school. (✓)
3 Oscar and Joao _____ to tidy their bedrooms. (✗)
4 Dario _____ the book back to Jose. (✓)
5 Frida and Sofia _____ a present for their friend Jana. (✓)
6 Hamid _____ his homework before dinner. (✓)
7 We _____ any food in the classroom. (✗)
8 We _____ our hands before we eat lunch. (✓)

4 ★★★ **Write five things you *must* or *mustn't* do this year.**

0 *I must learn a lot of new English words.*
1 _____
2 _____
3 _____
4 _____
5 _____

can (asking for permission)   → SB p.87

5 ★★☆ **Put the words in order to make questions.**

0 we / Can / the hockey match / Saturday / on / go / to
   Can we go to the hockey match on Saturday?
1 have / I / Can / chips / supper / for
   _____
2 I / Can / invite / Toby / to / my birthday party
   _____
3 go / we / Can / the park / to / school / after
   _____
4 phone / I / Can / my sister
   _____
5 I / wear / Can / green / jumper / your / today
   _____

6 ★★☆ **Match the children's questions with Dad's answers.**

0 *Can I take your laptop to school with me?*

1 *Can we go swimming on Sunday?*

2 *Can I go to Kate's house after school tonight?*

3 *Can Mike and I go climbing this weekend?*

a *No, we can't. The pool is closed this weekend.*

b *Yes, of course you can. But don't come home late.*

c *Well, OK. But be careful.*

d *No, you can't. I need it for work.*

I'd like … / Would you like …? → SB p.89

7 ★☆☆ **Write sentences using 'd like / Would … like.**

0 I / tomato soup
I'd like tomato soup.

1 my mum / steak and salad
_____

2 what / you / for dessert / ?
_____

3 Dad / ice cream for dessert / ?
_____

8 ★★☆ **Put the conversation in order.**

☐ **Waiter** (five minutes later) Are you ready to order?

☐ **Waiter** Four soups, OK. And what would you like for the main course?

☐ **Waiter** And finally, any drinks?

☐ **Waiter** OK, so would you like a starter?

1 **Waiter** Good evening. Would you like a table for four?

☐ **Customer** Yes, please.

☐ **Customer** Yes, we are.

☐ **Customer** Just water for everyone, thanks.

☐ **Customer** We'd like one cheese salad, one steak with potatoes and vegetables, one pizza and one burger and chips, please.

☐ **Customer** Yes, please. We'd like two tomato soups and two vegetable soups.

PRONUNCIATION
Intonation – giving two choices
Go to page 121. 🎧

9 ★★☆ **Look at the menu on page 88 of the Student's Book and complete the conversation so it is true for you.**

Waiter Are you ready to order?

You Yes, I am.

Waiter Would you like a starter?

You _____

Waiter And what would you like for the main course?

You _____

Waiter And would you like a dessert?

You _____

Waiter Any drinks?

You Yes, _____

GET IT RIGHT!

like and *would like*

We use *like* to say that something is nice.

✓ *I like ice cream. It's yummy!*

We use *would like* to ask for something we want or to ask somebody what they want.

✓ *I would like a burger, please.*

✗ *I like a burger, please.*

✓ *Would you like a burger?*

✗ *You like a burger?*

Circle the correct options.

0 I *like* / would like to come to your house tomorrow.

1 I *like* / *would like* a VR headset for my birthday.

2 I *like* / *would like* this house and I'm happy living here.

3 I *like* / *would like* travelling to different countries.

4 I *like* / *would like* to go shopping on Monday.

5 I'm thirsty. I *like* / *would like* a drink of water.

6 When I have time, I *like* / *would like* cooking.

VOCABULARY
Food and drink

→ SB p.86

1 ★☆☆ **Look at the pictures and complete the crossword. What's the mystery sentence?**

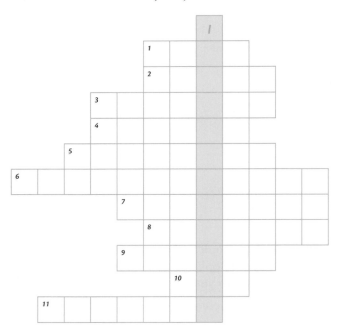

The mystery sentence is: _____

2 ★★☆ **Put the letters in order to make food words.**

0 We're having ___beef___ with potatoes and vegetables for lunch today. (e b e f)

1 My mum doesn't like _____ . (b l a m)

2 I often drink _____ with my breakfast. (l i m k)

3 I sometimes have an _____ after dinner. (p l p a e)

4 I'd like _____ and ice cream for dessert. (s t a r w b i r r e e s)

5 I like most vegetables, but I don't like _____ . (a c o r r t s)

Meals

→ SB p.89

3 ★☆☆ **Find and circle nine breakfast items in the word snake.**

abreadonbutterilkhoneymotoastljamogeggnyoghurtatcerealetfruitth

4 ★★☆ **Put the words in order to make sentences or questions.**

0 you / do / usually / eat / for / breakfast, / What / Dora / ?
What do you usually eat for breakfast, Dora?

1 always / I / eat / an / egg / breakfast / for
_____

2 usually / I / eat / toast
_____

3 you / lunch / usually / have / for / What / do / ?
_____

4 often / I / have / jacket potato / a
_____

5 sometimes / have / I / steak / chips / vegetables / and / with
_____

6 do / you / What / usually / drink / meals, / with / your / Dora / ?
_____

7 drink / I / usually / or water / fruit juice
_____

5 ★★☆ **Tick (✓) the things Dora has for breakfast and lunch in Exercise 4.**

☐ fruit   ☐ pizza   ☐ yoghurt
☐ toast   ☐ spaghetti   ☐ cereal
☐ an egg   ☐ vegetables   ☐ steak
☐ water   ☐ jacket potato   ☐ chicken
☐ coffee   ☐ fruit juice   ☐ chips

6 ★★★ **Write sentences about Luca and Jamie using the words in brackets.**

	always	often	sometimes	never
breakfast	an egg	toast	cereal	yoghurt
lunch	coffee	a sandwich	pizza	soup
dinner	soup	pasta	fish	salad

0 *They sometimes have cereal for breakfast.*
(sometimes)

1 _____ (always)

2 _____ (often)

3 _____ (never)

4 _____ (sometimes)

5 _____ (often)

REFERENCE

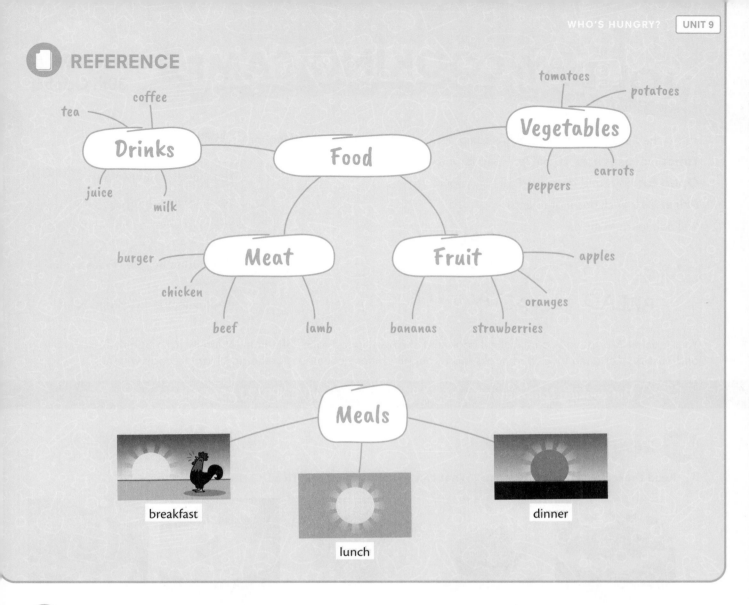

Drinks — tea, coffee, juice, milk

Food

Vegetables — tomatoes, potatoes, carrots, peppers

Meat — burger, chicken, beef, lamb

Fruit — apples, oranges, bananas, strawberries

Meals

breakfast

lunch

dinner

VOCABULARY *EXTRA*

1 Write the name of each food under the photos. Use words from the photos.

> cheese | cream | garlic | grapes | lemon | melon | onion

1 _____

2 _____

3 _____

4 _____

5 _____

6 _____

7 _____

2 Put the food from Exercise 1 into the correct category in the table.

dairy	fruit	vegetables
milk	apple	carrot

Mid-term HOLIDAY COOKING CAMP

28th, 29th & 30th October

This is the third year of our cooking camp. It's a great way to start cooking for yourself!

Time: mornings from 10 am to 1 pm, for three days

Open to: boys and girls aged 11–14 years

Price: £45 (includes ingredients)

You can learn to make:

CAKES PIZZA **HEALTHY SOUPS** FRUIT SMOOTHIES

BREAD **PASTA**

★ You must be 11–14 years old.

★ You must love food.

★ You must wear a chef's hat (don't worry, we give you one!).

★ You mustn't be late. There's a lot to learn.

★ And remember! Cooking is fun!

Your teacher Marianne is an excellent cook and she loves good food. She has got family from Spain, Turkey, Italy and Russia. Marianne loves and cooks food from all of those countries. Come and learn to cook with her.

Our cooking camps are very popular, so sign up now!! Call 0123 6564 to book your place.

READING

1 **Read the leaflet for Cooking camp. What can you learn to make? Tick (✓) the correct photos.**

 A

 B

 C

 D

 E

2 **Read the leaflet again and correct the sentences.**

0 Cooking camp is in November.
   Cooking camp is in October.

1 Cooking camp is for three afternoons.
   _____

2 You don't make any drinks.
   _____

3 Marianne has got family from Germany.
   _____

4 You must be 8–11 years old.
   _____

5 You mustn't wear any special clothes.
   _____

6 You mustn't be on time.
   _____

7 Remember that cooking is important.
   _____

3 CRITICAL THINKING **Answer the questions about the food camp.**

1 What things on the list are healthy things to cook?

2 Can you think of one reason why cooking is fun?

3 Think of two reasons why it is important for young people to learn to cook.

4 **Complete the questionnaire for the Cooking camp so it is true for you.**

COOKING CAMP
Questionnaire

★ 1 What's your name? _____

★ 2 How old are you? _____

★ 3 What is your favourite dish? _____

★ 4 Do you help your parents in the kitchen? _____

★ 5 Can you cook? _____

★ 6 What can you cook? _____

DEVELOPING Writing

My birthday meal plan

1 **INPUT** **Read the text about Samu's birthday dinner. What does he never drink on his birthday?**

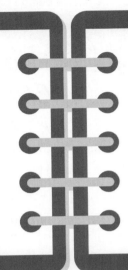

> My family usually eats healthy food, like rice and meat with vegetables, and fruit for dessert. But on my birthday, we always have a special dinner together. We sometimes have my mum's amazing pizza, and sometimes chicken with hot sauce, chips and salad (my favourite!). For dessert, we have my favourite ice cream – strawberry. My mum always makes my birthday cake. It's usually chocolate cake with cream. I never drink cola on my birthday. I like lemonade.

2 **ANALYSE** **Answer the questions.**

0 How often does Samu's family eat healthy food?
They usually eat healthy food.

1 What is his favourite birthday meal?
_____

2 What does he have for dessert on his birthday?
_____

3 What does his mother always make him?
_____

4 What does he usually drink on his birthday?
_____

3 **PLAN** **Think about a dinner your family often eats on normal days. Now plan a special birthday meal with your favourite foods. Write your food choices in the table. Use words from the list and your own ideas.**

bread | burger | chicken | chips | chocolate
chocolate cake | cola | eggs | fish | fruit
fruit juice | ice cream | jacket potato
meat | milk | pasta | pizza | rice | salad
soup | toast | vegetables | water

	normal meal	special birthday meal
food and drink	_____	_____
	_____	_____
	_____	_____
	_____	_____
	_____	_____

4 **PRODUCE** **Use your notes from Exercise 3 to write a birthday meal plan. Use the text in Exercise 1 to help you. Write about 60 words.**

_____
_____
_____
_____
_____
_____
_____
_____
_____
_____
_____
_____
_____

WRITING TIP: Adding detail

Add more detail to your writing by using adverbs of frequency:

• How often do you eat things?

You can answer this question with *always, usually, sometimes* and *never.*

I sometimes have my mum's pizza.
I never drink cola.
I usually have fruit for dessert.
I always have a special birthday lunch with my family.

 **LISTENING**

1 🔊 9.02 **Listen and tick (✓) the things on the menu that the family decide to order.**

The BURGER and SALAD BAR
MENU

STARTERS
Soup of the day* ☐

Salad bar ☐

MAIN COURSE
Our delicious **burgers**!

★ Beef ☐ ★ Lamb ☐ ★ Vegetable ☐

Our amazing **grills**!

★ Chicken ☐ ★ Steak ☐ ★ Fish ☐

SIDES
Chips ☐

Jacket potato ☐

Vegetables of the day * ☐

Onion rings ☐

DRINKS
Lemonade ☐

Cola ☐

Apple juice ☐

Orange juice ☐

Pot of tea ☐

Coffee ☐

Water ☐

DESSERT
Chef's dessert of the day * ☐

Carrot cake ☐

Ice cream:

★ Strawberry ☐ ★ Chocolate ☐ ★ Vanilla ☐

Look at the board on the wall!

2 🔊 9.02 **Listen again and mark the sentences T (true) or F (false).**

0 You choose your own food at the salad bar. ☐ T

1 The soup of the day is tomato. ☐

2 Kabir loves broccoli and carrots. ☐

3 Kabir orders three things. ☐

4 Dad doesn't want a starter. ☐

5 Aisha has a small dessert. ☐

DIALOGUE

3 (Circle) **the correct options.**

Waiter	Are you ready to ⁰sit down / order?
Customer 1	Yes, we are.
Waiter	Would you like a ¹starter / main course?
Customer 1	Yes, please. I'd like tomato soup.
Customer 2	And I'd like vegetable soup.
Waiter	And what would you like for the ²dessert / main course?
Customer 1	I'd like chicken salad, please.
Customer 2	And I'd like fish and chips, please.
Waiter	And for ³starter / dessert?
Customer 1	We'd like the chocolate cake, please.
Waiter	Any ⁴drinks / desserts?
Customer 1	Yes, please. I'd like apple juice.
Customer 2	And I'd like water.

PHRASES FOR FLUENCY → SB p.90

4 **Complete the conversations with phrases from the list.**

> Of course. | Be careful! | a bit of | the thing is

Conversation 1

A Can you take these plates to the table?

B OK.

A _____ Don't drop them.

B It's OK Dad. Don't worry!

Conversation 2

A What's for dinner?

B It's pizza.

A Oh, no.

B What's wrong with pizza? I love it.

A Well, _____ , I don't like tomatoes.

Conversation 3

A Is there any cheese on the jacket potato?

B Yes, there is and there's _____ butter, too.

Conversation 4

A Would you like some vegetables with your steak?

B _____ I love vegetables.

SUM IT UP

1 Put the letters in order to find the food words.

What's on Mario's pizza?

0 s e e c h e   *cheese*

1 r e p s p e p   _____

2 k i c e n c h   _____

3 o e s t o m t a   _____

What would Evalina like for dinner?

4 k e a s t   _____

5 t o p o e s t a   _____

6 d a s a l   _____

What's in Emre's dessert?

7 c o c h l a t e o   _____

8 c i e r e c a m   _____

9 r a w s t e r r i e b s   _____

10 n a b a n a   _____

C A F É _____

_____

starters

_____

_____

drinks

_____

_____

main courses

_____

_____

_____

desserts

_____

_____

_____

2 Complete the menu. Use food and drink words from the unit.

- Think of a name for your café.
- Create a milkshake or a smoothie.
- Make a special pizza for your café.
- Create meals with the food words.
- Create one unusual meal.

For example: *Strawberry and Orange Salad* or *Carrot and Orange Soup*

3 Imagine you have a customer at your café. Complete the conversation.

Waiter   Hello and welcome to [1]_____ Café.

Customer 1   Hello. We'd like a table for two.

Waiter   OK. Follow me, please.

(5 minutes later)

Waiter   Are you ready to order now?

Customer 1   Yes, we are.

Waiter   Would you like a starter?

Customer 1   Yes, please. [2]_____ and my friend [3]_____ .

Waiter   And what [4]_____ for the main course?

Customer 1   [5]_____ , please.

Customer 2   And [6]_____ .

Waiter   And for dessert?

Customer 1   [7]_____ , please.

Customer 2   And [8]_____ .

Waiter   Any drinks?

Customer 1   Yes, please. [9]_____ and my friend [10]_____ .

10 BIG SUCCESSES

Grammar rap!

▶29

Ⓖ GRAMMAR

Past simple: *was / wasn't; were / weren't; there was / were* → SB p.94

1 ⭐☆☆ **Circle the correct options.**

0 You *was* / *were* late.

1 It *wasn't* / *weren't* his book.

2 I *was* / *were* at home yesterday.

3 We *was* / *were* at the cinema.

4 They *wasn't* / *weren't* at the hockey match last night.

5 She *was* / *were* my best friend.

2 ⭐⭐☆ **Complete the sentences with *was, were, wasn't* or *weren't*.**

0 I _____was_____ (✓) born in Mexico City.

1 My grandma _____ (✗) a pilot.

2 Arlo and Jay _____ (✓) in the park yesterday.

3 We _____ (✗) at my aunt's house last night.

4 Leon _____ (✗) at the basketball court on Sunday.

5 It _____ (✓) my birthday yesterday.

3 ⭐⭐⭐ **Complete the text with the correct past simple form of *to be*.**

The Montgolfier brothers ⁰____were____ the inventors of the hot-air balloon. They ¹_____ (✓) French. Their names ²_____ (✓) Joseph-Michel and Jacques-Étienne. Joseph-Michel ³_____ (✓) born in 1740, and Jacques-Étienne ⁴_____ (✓) born in 1745. There ⁵_____ (✓) sixteen children in the family. Their father ⁶_____ (✗) an inventor. He ⁷_____ (✓) a paper manufacturer. The first balloon flight ⁸_____ (✓) in June 1783. There ⁹_____ (✗) any passengers. There ¹⁰_____ (✓) no one on the balloon. The second flight ¹¹_____ (✓) in Paris in September 1783. This time, there ¹²_____ (✓) three passengers, but the passengers ¹³_____ (✗) people. They ¹⁴_____ (✓) a chicken, a duck and a sheep.

Past simple: *Was he …? / Were you …?* → SB p.95

4 ⭐☆☆ **Match the questions with the answers.**

0 Were you born in Rome?

1 Was your grandfather a chef?

2 Was Valentina an astronaut?

3 Was it your phone?

4 Was I late to the party?

5 Were you and I on time?

6 Were Sandro and Joel at the youth club yesterday?

a No, he wasn't.

b Yes, you were!

c Yes, it was.

d No, we weren't.

e Yes, I was.

f No, they weren't.

g Yes, she was.

5 ⭐⭐⭐ **Put the words in order to make questions. Then look at the text in Exercise 3 and answer the questions.**

0 Were / the / inventors / brothers / Montgolfier

Were the Montgolfier brothers inventors?

Yes, they were.

1 they / Italian / Were

_____

_____

2 Was / Joseph-Michel / in 1740 / born

_____

_____

3 Was / inventor / an / their / father

_____

_____

4 the / Was / in / flight / first / June 1795

_____

_____

5 flight / second / Prague / in / Was / the

_____

_____

6 Were / there / passengers / any

_____

_____

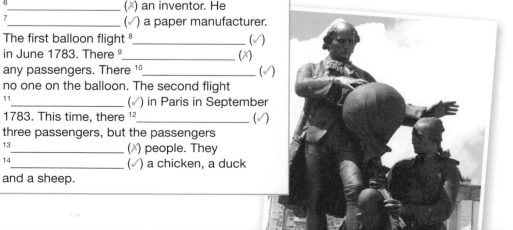

Past simple: regular verbs → SB p.97

6 ★☆☆ **Complete the table with the correct past simple of the verbs in the list.**

believe | carry | cry | finish
help | like | live | study | work

+ -ed	+ -d	+ -ied
finished		

7 ★★☆ **Put the words in order to make sentences. Put the verbs in the past simple.**

0 uncle / My / study / university / at / medicine
   My uncle studied medicine at university.

1 finish / degree / his / He / 2010 / in
   _____

2 at / hospital / a / He / work / Birmingham / in
   _____

3 in / He / Madrid / three / years / for / live
   _____

4 like / He / Spain / very / much
   _____

5 move / He / London / to / 2014 / in
   _____

8 ★★☆ **Complete the text with the past simple form of the verbs in brackets.**

DAVID ATTENBOROUGH

The famous scientist David Attenborough
0 _lived_ (live) in London as a child.
He 1_____ (study) at Cambridge University, and later in London. In 1950, Attenborough 2_____ (marry) Jane Oriel and they had two children. He 3_____ (work) for the BBC for many years as a producer, but he 4_____ (want) to make programmes about nature. In 1972, he 5_____ (stop) working at the BBC and 6_____ (start) to make nature programmes. He soon 7_____ (return) to the BBC and made many famous series, including *Life on Earth* in 1976, with 96 episodes! Over many years, Attenborough and his teams 8_____ (discover) new ways to film animals and plants. He 9_____ (travel) to all seven continents, and millions of people 10_____ (watch) his programmes.

9 ★★★ **Complete the text with the past simple form of the verbs in brackets.**

Florence Nightingale

Florence Nightingale 0 _was_ (be) a famous English nurse. She 1_____ (be) born in Florence, Italy, in 1820. Later, her parents 2_____ (move) back to England. As a child, she 3_____ (like) helping others. She 4_____ (care) for sick people and animals. She 5_____ (want) to be a nurse. In 1851, she 6_____ (work) as a nurse in Germany. In 1853, there 7_____ (be) a war. It 8_____ (be) called the Crimean War. They 9_____ (need) nurses, so Florence 10_____ (sail) with nurses to help. They 11_____ (look) after the British soldiers there. Life 12_____ (not be) easy. The war 13_____ (end) in 1856. Florence Nightingale 14_____ (return) to England as a hero. She 15_____ (die) in London in 1910.

PRONUNCIATION
Past simple regular verbs Go to page 121.

GET IT RIGHT!

was / wasn't* and *were / weren't
We use *was, wasn't, were* and *weren't* to talk about the past. We use *am, am not, is, isn't, are* and *aren't* to talk about now.
✓ *Yesterday was my birthday.*
✗ *Yesterday is my birthday.*
Correct the sentences.
0 Geoff isn't at school yesterday.
   Geoff wasn't at school yesterday.
1 There is a great film on TV last night.
   _____
2 Hello! I was very happy to see you.
   _____
3 All my friends are there for my birthday last night.
   _____
4 Is Laura with you yesterday evening?
   _____
5 Gioia was worried about her exam today.
   _____
6 They aren't late for school yesterday.
   _____

VOCABULARY
Time expressions: past

→ SB p.94

1 ★☆☆ **Complete the table with the words from the list.**

afternoon | evening | ~~month~~
morning | night | Saturday
three o'clock | year | 6 pm
10.30 | 1969 | 2015

last	in
month	
at	**yesterday**

2 ★☆☆ **Complete the dialogues with *at, in, last* and *yesterday*.**

0 **A** Where were you _____*last*_____ night?
   B I was at home.

1 **A** Were you at school _____ afternoon?
   B Yes, I was.

2 **A** Was Jaime at the party _____ Saturday?
   B No, he was at home.

3 **A** Was your dad born _____ 1980?
   B No, he wasn't.

4 **A** Was Tim still at school _____ 5 pm this evening?
   B Yes, he was.

3 ★★☆ **Where were you? Write sentences with *at, last* and *yesterday* and the time if necessary.**

0 (at) *I was on the bus at eight o'clock.*
   _____

1 (at) _____
   _____

2 (last) _____
   _____

3 (yesterday) _____
   _____

The weather

→ SB p.97

4 ★★☆ **Complete the sentences and the crossword with the same words.**

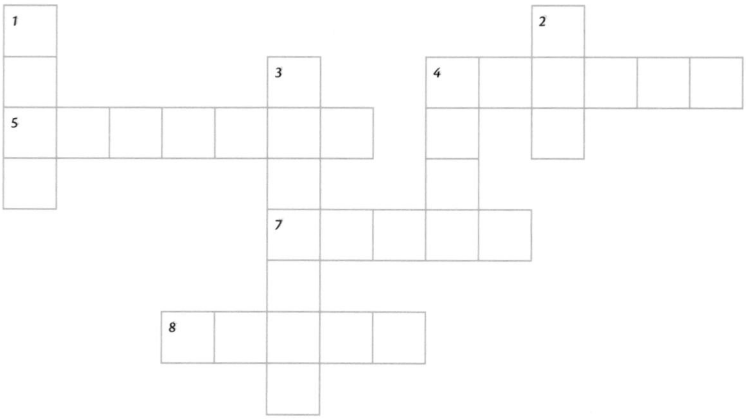

[crossword grid with numbered cells 1, 2, 3, 4, 5, 7, 8]

ACROSS

4 Today it's _____ , so we don't need our sunglasses.

5 It's _____ , so don't forget your umbrella.

7 It's _____ , so it's a great day to fly your kite.

8 It's _____ – there are lots of people on the beach today.

DOWN

1 Today is lovely and _____ . Let's sit outside.

2 Drink lots of water today – it's very _____ !

3 You can make a snowman today. It's _____ .

4 It's _____ today, so don't forget to wear warm clothes.

5 ★★☆ (Circle) **the correct options in these phone conversations.**

1 **A** What's the weather like?
   B It's ⁰(sunny) / cloudy. I'm wearing sunglasses.
   A Is it ¹cold / hot?
   B Yes, it is. I'm wearing a T-shirt. What's the weather like there?
   A It's very ²cloudy / windy here. Listen. Can you hear it?
   B Yes, I can.

2 **A** What's the weather like?
   B It's ³raining / cloudy. I can't play football outside today.
   A Is it ⁴cold / hot?
   B Yes, it is. I'm wearing a jumper and a coat. What's the weather like there?
   A It's ⁵snowing / windy here. We can't go to school today because we can't get out of the house.
   B Really?

6 ★★★ **Write sentences about the weather today. What can or can't you do?**

_____
_____
_____
_____

REFERENCE

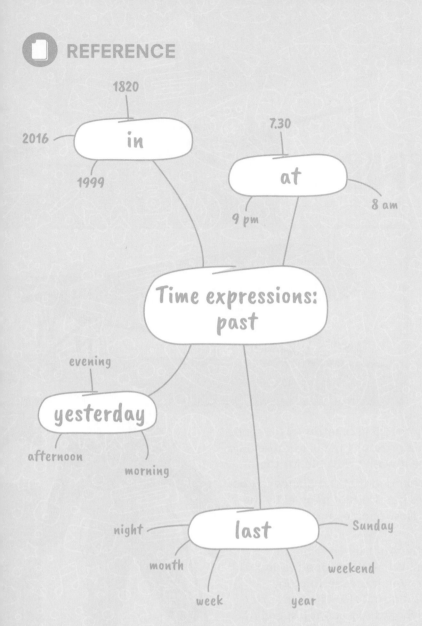

1820
in
2016
1999

7.30
at
9 pm
8 am

Time expressions: past

evening
yesterday
afternoon
morning

night
last
Sunday
month
weekend
week
year

The weather

It's sunny.

It's cloudy.

It's hot.

It's raining.

It's snowing.

It's windy.

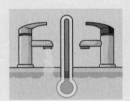
It's cold.

It's warm.

 # VOCABULARY *EXTRA*

1 Match the definitions with the words from the list.

after | ~~at noon~~ | at midnight | before | early | late

0 in the middle of the day: _at noon_

1 before something starts: _____

2 earlier than something else: _____

3 after something starts: _____

4 at 12 o'clock at night: _____

5 in the time following something else: _____

2 Put the letters in order to make words.

0 Please don't be ___late___ for the film. We mustn't miss the beginning! (a l t e)

1 My little sister's birthday in June is _____ my birthday in May. (t e f a r)

2 Can you come _____ the party starts to help me with the food? (e o e r f b)

3 The music festival starts _____ on Saturday. (t a o n o n)

4 To get a good seat at the concert, you need to arrive very _____ (e y l r a)

5 The last bus home from the town centre is _____ (t a d g h i i m n t)

Flying MACHINES

A

Do you like flying? Did you know that there are different ways to explore the skies? Here we look at two incredible flying inventions from France!

On 25th July 1909, the French aviator Louis Blériot flew a monoplane (a plane with one pair of wings) across the English Channel - the sea between France and England. He developed the first monoplane with a pilot, and he was the first person to fly from one country to another across the sea! The plane didn't look very strong, but it only took 36 minutes and 30 seconds to fly the 35 kilometres from France to England. An English newspaper gave him a prize of £1,000. In those days, most people only dreamed of flying, because it wasn't possible for them.

B

The invention of the jet plane in the 1930s changed that. Jet planes can go very fast, for a long way, and with sometimes hundreds of people. By the 1960s, air travel as we know it was possible. Now people, and not just rich people, fly all over the world.

And inventors are still finding new ways to fly! Another Frenchman, Franky Zapata, was a jet ski World Champion. When he stopped racing, he invented a hoverboard called the Flyboard Air. It uses technology similar to drones, and jet plane fuel. On 4th August 2019, 110 years after Blériot, Zapata crossed the Channel on his Flyboard Air, at a top speed of 170 kilometres an hour, and arrived safely on the south coast of England in 22 minutes. He looked like a superhero in a comic!

Can you imagine people on hoverboards flying everywhere in the future? Who knows! In 1909, no one imagined people flying away on holiday! How quickly things change!

C

📖 READING

1 **Read the article about flying machines. Put the photos in order from old to new (1–3).**

2 **Read the article again. What do these numbers mean?**

0 2019 *Franky Zapata crossed the Channel on the Flyboard Air.*
1 35 _____
2 1909 _____
3 22 _____
4 1,000 _____
5 170 _____

3 CRITICAL THINKING **Read the article again and tick (✓) the words you think describe Zapata's hoverboard. Why did you choose each word? Write your reasons.**

- fun ☐
- expensive ☐
- dangerous ☐
- climate-friendly ☐
- easy to use ☐
- a great idea ☐

_____
_____
_____
_____

DEVELOPING Writing

A short biography

1 **INPUT** **Read the fact file and biography of Alicia Keys. Where was she born?**

A Personal details

Alicia Keys is an American singer, pianist and songwriter. Her real name is Alicia Augello-Cook. She was born in New York on 25th January 1981 and lived in a poor area. She is married to a DJ, Swizz Beatz, and they have two sons.

B Professional

Alicia went to the Professional Performing Arts School in New York, and studied classical piano. A record company gave her a contract when she was only 15. She has many hit songs and successful albums.

C Charity work

Alicia helped start a charity in Africa, called Keep a Child Alive, which helps sick children, and she organises concerts to raise money every year. She also tries to help fight racism and poverty.

FACT FILE

Alicia Keys

1 Date of birth: 25th January 1981

2 Nationality: American

3 Education: Professional Performing Arts School, New York

4 Real name: Alicia Augello-Cook

5 Family: married to DJ Swizz Beatz, two sons

6 Place of birth: New York

7 Job: singer, musician, songwriter

8 Big break: Record contract in 1996, aged 15

9 Charity work: Keep a Child Alive (charity in Africa, helps sick children)

2 **ANALYSE** **Match sections 1–9 in the fact file with paragraphs A–C.**

Paragraph A: Section(s): _____

Paragraph B: Section(s): _____

Paragraph C: Section(s): _____

3 **Read paragraphs A and B again and find three facts that are not in the fact file. Then match them with the correct sections in the fact file.**

4 **PLAN** **Use the information in the list to complete the fact file about Millie Bobby Brown.**

actress, producer | British | Millie Bobby Brown
2016, Eleven in *Stranger Things*, aged 12
Marbella, Spain (now lives in the US)
Millie Bobby Brown | 19th February 2004
two sisters, one brother
UNICEF ambassador (youngest ever)

FACT FILE

Millie Bobby Brown

1 Nationality:

2 Place of birth:

3 Date of birth:

4 Real name:

5 Family:

6 Job:

7 Big break:

8 Charity work:

✏ WRITING TIP: Organisation

A biography includes a lot of information, so it needs good organisation.

One way to do this is with paragraphs and headings, like in the text about Alicia Keys:

- A Personal details
- B Professional
- C Charity work

5 **PRODUCE** **Use the fact file to write a short biography of Millie Bobby Brown. You can use the internet to find more information. Write about 70 words.**

🎧 LISTENING

1 Look at the picture and guess the answers to the questions.

1 Who is the man in the photo?

_____

2 What did he write about?

_____

2 🔊 10.02 **Listen to Tom talking about a writer. Circle the correct options.**

0 Tom's hero was a (writer) / artist.

1 His most famous book was *Narnia* / *The Jungle Book*.

2 His parents were *English* / *Indian*.

3 His father was *a doctor* / *an artist*.

4 Rudyard Kipling *loved* / *hated* India.

5 He was *happy* / *unhappy* with the Holloways.

6 He *loved* / *hated* books.

7 He was *happy* / *unhappy* at school in Devon.

8 After school he lived in *Italy* / *India*.

9 He worked for a *newspaper* / *university*.

3 🔊 10.02 **Listen again and complete the text with the correct words.**

Rudyard Kipling's parents were English. They ⁰___*moved*___ to India. His father was an artist and he worked at a School of Art in Mumbai. Kipling loved India. He loved the ¹_____ and the culture. However, he didn't have a happy childhood. His parents wanted him to go to ²_____ in England. When he was six years old, he lived with a ³_____ , the Holloways, in a seaside ⁴_____ in England. Mrs Holloway was very bad to him. He ⁵_____ life there and he was very unhappy. Luckily, he ⁶_____ books. He loved books. They ⁷_____ him from his unhappy life.

DIALOGUE

4 Complete the conversation with the past simple of the verbs in brackets. Then put the conversation in order.

☐1 **Ben** ⁰___*Were*___ (be) you at home yesterday?

☐ **Ben** Did they? ¹_____ (be) they good?

☐ **Ben** ²_____ (be) it a good party?

☐ **Ben** Oh, I remember. It ³_____ (be) your cousin's birthday yesterday, right?

☐ **Sam** Yes, they ⁴_____ (be) very good.

☐ **Sam** Yes, it ⁵_____ (be). I loved it.

☐ **Sam** Yes, it ⁶_____ (be). Her brothers are in a band. They ⁷_____ (play) at her party.

☐ **Sam** No, I ⁸_____ (not be). I ⁹_____ (be) at my cousin's house.

Train to TH!NK

Sequencing

5 Complete the sequence with words from the list.

And then | Finally | First

> _____ > Then > _____
> After that > _____

6 Order the events in Rudyard Kipling's life. Then complete the sentences with sequencing words from Exercise 5.

Rudyard Kipling (1865–1936)

☐ _____ , he died in London in 1936.

☐ _____ he lived in a seaside town in England with the Holloway family.

☐ _____*First*_____ , Rudyard Kipling lived in India.

☐ _____ he moved to a school in Devon.

☐ _____ , he moved back to India and he worked for a newspaper.

EXAM SKILLS: LISTENING
Listening for key words

1   🔊 10.03   **Listen and tick (✓) the months you hear.**

> January ☐ | February ☐ | March ☐ | April ☐ | May ☐ | June ☐ | July ☐
> August ☐ | September ☐ | October ☐ | November ☐ | December ☐

 **LISTENING TIP**

- First, learn to listen for key words, for example, the months of the year.
- Next, you need to complete the profile. Listen carefully for the dates, the jobs and the places.

Remember! You don't need to understand everything.

2   🔊 10.04   **Listen and circle the correct options to complete Claude Monet's profile.**

Claude Monet

0 Job
writer / *painter*

1 Nationality
French / Italian

2 Born
14th *September / November* 1840

3 Mother's job
singer / actor

4 Father's job
gardener / grocer

5 September 1870
He lived in *London / New York.*

6 May 1871
He moved to *Germany / Holland.*

7 May 1883
He moved to Giverny in *France / Belgium.*

8 Died
5th *June / December* 1926

3   🔊 10.05   **Listen and complete Vincent Van Gogh's profile.**

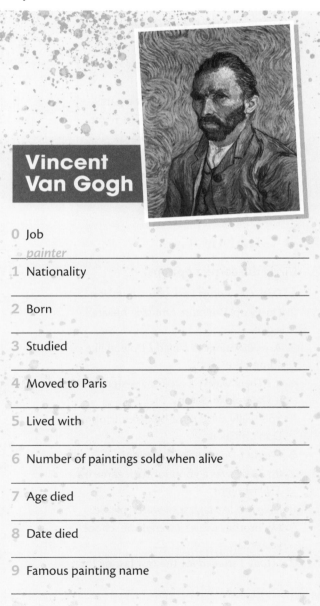

Vincent Van Gogh

0 Job
painter

1 Nationality
_____

2 Born
_____

3 Studied
_____

4 Moved to Paris
_____

5 Lived with
_____

6 Number of paintings sold when alive
_____

7 Age died
_____

8 Date died
_____

9 Famous painting name
_____

CONSOLIDATION

🎧 LISTENING

1 🔊 **10.06** **Listen to Charlotte and Jack and circle the correct answers (A, B or C).**

1 For breakfast, Charlotte doesn't want …
  A orange juice.
  B cereal.
  C eggs.

2 Charlotte arrived home at …
  A eleven o'clock.
  B twelve o'clock.
  C one o'clock.

3 Charlotte wants to read her …
  A emails.
  B newspaper.
  C tablet.

2 🔊 **10.06** **Listen again. Mark the sentences T (true) or F (false).**

1 Charlotte wants yoghurt for breakfast. ☐
2 She wants tea. ☐
3 Last night, Charlotte was at a party. ☐
4 Jack worked for five hours last night. ☐
5 Jack says he always works hard. ☐
6 The weather is rainy and cold. ☐
7 Charlotte wants to borrow Jack's tablet. ☐
8 Charlotte is going to work. ☐

⚙ GRAMMAR

3 **Circle the correct options.**

1 Dad, *can / must* I ask you a question?
2 Hurry up! We *must / mustn't* be late again.
3 Are you hungry? *Would / Do* you like some cake?
4 *It / There* wasn't a nice day yesterday. It was cold and rainy.
5 You really *can / must* be careful, John. Don't break it!
6 *Would / Do* you like this song?
7 *It / There* was a good football game on TV last night.
8 *I like / I'd like* a glass of water, please.
9 My brother *wasn't / weren't* at school yesterday.
10 I *study / studied* for the test last night.

4 **Complete the sentences with the correct form of verbs from the list.**

> arrive | be (x2) | like | not be (x2) | rain
> show | stay | travel | want | watch

Our holiday last year wasn't very good! We
¹_____ to Wales by car. We ²_____ very late
and the man at the hotel ³_____ angry with us.
Then he ⁴_____ us the rooms. They ⁵_____
really small and cold. We ⁶_____ to change the
rooms but the man said that there ⁷_____ any
other rooms. We ⁸_____ in the hotel for three
nights. The weather ⁹_____ good. It ¹⁰_____
almost all the time! One day, I stayed in my room and
¹¹_____ TV for about six hours. But the food was
good. We ¹²_____ it a lot. Next year, we don't
want to go to that hotel again.

🔤 VOCABULARY

5 **Complete the words.**

1 Do you want black coffee, or coffee with m __ __ k?
2 It's cold and w __ __ __ y today.
3 I don't eat a lot of v __ __ __ __ __ __ __ __ s.
4 My favourite fruit is an o __ __ __ __ __ __ .
5 I was at home yesterday e __ __ __ __ __ g.
6 It was her birthday last M __ __ __ h.
7 There's no sun today – it's very c __ __ __ __ y.
8 I watched tennis yesterday a __ __ __ __ __ __ __ n.
9 I'd like apple juice and eggs for b __ __ __ __ __ __ __ t.
10 I love eating b __ __ __ __ __ s and chips.

6 **Complete the dialogue with words from the list.**

> dinner | fruit | meat | night | o'clock
> potatoes | strawberries | tea

Liam What time do you usually eat in your family?
Nicky Well, we usually have lunch at one ⁰_____*o'clock*_____ .
And then we have ¹_____ at eight in the
evening.
Liam And what do you eat in the evening?
Nicky We have ²_____ – beef or chicken –
and some vegetables, for example, carrots or
³_____ . I usually drink juice, but my parents
like hot drinks, so they have ⁴_____ .
Liam And then?
Nicky Then we have ⁵_____ , usually apples, but
last ⁶_____ we had ⁷_____ –
they're my favourite!

DIALOGUE

7 🔊 10.07 **Complete the dialogue with the words from the list. There are two extra words. Then listen and check.**

> bit | can | careful | course | liked | mustn't | thing | wanted | was | wasn't | were | weren't

Clara So, what was Jason's party like last night?

Giorgio It was great. We all enjoyed it. There ¹_____ great music and I danced a lot. And all my friends were there.

Clara Was there any food?

Giorgio Yes. There ²_____ sandwiches and cheese, and some really nice chicken wings, too. The ³_____ is …

Clara Yes?

Giorgio Well, Jason's mum cooked some risotto and it ⁴_____ good at all! No one ⁵_____ it. At the end of the party, it was all still there! I usually love risotto, but not that!

Clara Oh, dear. Oh, look. Jason's coming. Be ⁶_____ ! We ⁷_____ say anything about the risotto, OK?

Giorgio No, sure. Jason! Hi. How are you? Thanks for the party!

Jason Hi, Giorgio. Hi, Clara. No problem. I'm happy that you enjoyed it. But Giorgio, ⁸_____ I ask you something?

Giorgio Er, of ⁹_____ . What?

Jason My mum's risotto. Was it really terrible? No one ¹⁰_____ to eat it!

Clara Go on, Giorgio. I think you can tell him!

📖 READING

8 **Read Emily's email. Then correct the sentences.**

1 Yesterday was Emily's fourteenth birthday.
   _____

2 The restaurant only serves Thai food.
   _____

3 The restaurant was noisy.
   _____

4 Emily didn't like the soup.
   _____

5 Emily's mother and father don't eat fish.
   _____

6 Emily's family eat in restaurants a lot.
   _____

7 There was writing on the candles.
   _____

8 Emily's family is having dessert at a restaurant tonight.
   _____

✏️ WRITING

9 **Write a paragraph about a good or bad meal you remember. Write about 60 words. Use the questions to help you.**

- Where were you?
- What was the meal? (dinner? lunch?)
- Who was there?
- What was the food?
- Why was it a good/bad meal?

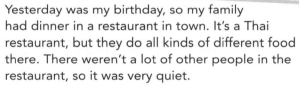

⭐ **Alli**
Emily@thinkmail.com

Hi Alli,

Yesterday was my birthday, so my family had dinner in a restaurant in town. It's a Thai restaurant, but they do all kinds of different food there. There weren't a lot of other people in the restaurant, so it was very quiet.

The dinner was really nice. We started with vegetable soup – it was delicious! Then I ordered beef with peppers and mushrooms. My parents ordered fish (they don't eat meat) with peanut sauce and rice. And for dessert, I had banana and mango ice cream, my favourite! The food was great – I enjoyed my meal a lot. We don't usually eat in restaurants, so it was a special evening.

When we finished eating, a waiter came over with a big birthday cake! It had thirteen candles on it (of course!) and the words 'Happy Birthday Emily' in big letters in the middle. The waiters and my parents started to sing 'Happy Birthday to you' and the other people in the restaurant joined in, too. At the end of the song, everyone clapped – it was really nice! There was enough cake for us and the other people in the restaurant, and there's some in the fridge in our kitchen now!

So, dessert at our house tonight is birthday cake!

Love,

Emily

Grammar rap!

ⓖ GRAMMAR
Past simple: irregular verbs
→ SB p.104

1 ★☆☆ **Complete the table with the past simple or the base form of the verbs.**

base form	past simple
0 ran	*ran*
1	came
2	put
3 give	
4 see	
5	knew
6	drank
7 fall	
8 write	
9	took
10 eat	

2 ★★☆ **Complete the text with the past simple form of the verbs in brackets.**

The Hill family's holiday

Last year, the Hill family from Scotland decided to have a holiday in England. They ⁰___*went*___ (go) to the west of England. Mr Hill ¹_____ (make) a reservation at a hotel in Bath. In Bath, they ²_____ (see) the Roman baths and the city centre. Then Margot ³_____ (find) Longleat Safari Park on her computer. She ⁴_____ (tell) her parents about the old house and the park with lions, gorillas and lots of other animals. The website ⁵_____ (say) it was the first safari park outside Africa. All the family ⁶_____ (think) it was a good idea to visit the park. So they ⁷_____ (get) in the car and ⁸_____ (drive) to Longleat. They ⁹_____ (have) a really good time there!

Past simple (negative)
→ SB p.104

3 ★★★ **Write sentences about a birthday party. Use the past simple negative.**

0 my grandmother / to the party (come)
   My grandmother didn't come to the party.

1 the band / classical music (play)
   _____

2 we / bread and butter (eat)
   _____

3 Adriana / me a dictionary (give)
   _____

4 Mum / my dress (make)
   _____

5 Rob / a spider on the table (see)
   _____

6 my father / us home (take)
   _____

7 Stefan / a snake in a box (find)
   _____

8 we / a film (watch)
   _____

4 ★★☆ **Logan didn't have a good weekend. Complete the sentences with the past simple form of the verbs in the list.**

> be | be | decide | do | not do | not rain
> not work | rain | try | use | want

0 Last weekend _____*was*_____ awful.
1 It _____ all day on Saturday.
2 I _____ anything interesting.
3 I _____ to watch a film but the download _____ .
4 My brother _____ the computer for his homework all afternoon.
5 I _____ to go out but it was too cold and wet.
6 But, it _____ on Sunday. Great!
7 So I _____ to ride my bike to the park.
8 But my bike _____ broken.
9 What _____ you _____ last weekend?

5 ⭐⭐⭐ Complete the text with the past simple form of a verb in the box.

> eat | go | go | have | not be | not like
> not want | not watch | see | share | spend | take

Sarah ⁰_____went_____ to London last weekend with three friends. They stayed in a student hotel. It was very cheap, but the rooms ¹_____ very nice. Sarah ²_____ a room with Lisa. The hotel has a café and on Friday evening they ³_____ there because they were tired from the journey. But Craig and Alex ⁴_____ the pizza very much. On Saturday morning, Sarah and Alex ⁵_____ to the Natural History Museum in South Kensington. They ⁶_____ a dodo and a mammoth. Craig and Lisa ⁷_____ to look at animals, so they ⁸_____ the morning in the Science Museum instead. In the evening, they ⁹_____ the tube to Leicester Square but they ¹⁰_____ a film because all the cinemas were very expensive. So they ¹¹_____ a burger and this time the boys were happy!

Past simple (questions) → SB p.105

6 ⭐⭐⭐ Use the information in Exercise 5 and write questions about Sarah for these answers.

0 A *Where did Sarah go last weekend?*
  B She went to London.
1 A Where _____
  B In a hotel.
2 A What _____on Friday?
  B A pizza in the café.
3 A Where _____
  B In the Natural History Museum.
4 A What _____
  B A dodo and a mammoth.
5 A What _____
  B A burger.

> **PRONUNCIATION**
> Short vowel sound /ʊ/ Go to page 121. 🎧

could / couldn't (ability) → SB p.107

7 ⭐⭐☆ Last year, Ben broke his leg and they put it in plaster. What could he do? What couldn't he do? Use phrases from the list.

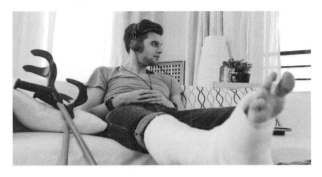

> do his homework | eat a pizza | go swimming
> listen to music | ~~play football~~ | play the guitar
> ride a bike | text his friends | ~~watch TV~~

0 *Ben could watch TV.*
0 *He couldn't play football.*
1 He _____
2 He _____
3 He _____
4 He _____
5 He _____
6 He _____
7 He _____

GET IT RIGHT!

Past simple

We always use the base form of the verb after *didn't* (in negative sentences) or *Did* (in questions).
✓ I didn't go to the party last Saturday.
✗ ~~I didn't went to the party last Saturday.~~
✓ Did you visit the Science Museum?
✗ ~~Did you visited the Science Museum?~~

Correct the sentences.
0 He didn't finished his homework.
  He didn't finish his homework.
1 Jack didn't liked the party.
  _____
2 We didn't paid much for lunch at the zoo yesterday.
  _____
3 Did they enjoyed their holiday?
  _____
4 We didn't knew where it was but finally we found it.
  _____
5 Billy's friend didn't ate a lot of food yesterday.
  _____
6 Did you went to the party?
  _____

VOCABULARY
Verb and noun pairs

→ SB p.104

1 ★★☆ **Read the sentences. Are the underlined words correct (✓) or incorrect (✗)? Write the correct words.**

0 I always <u>do</u> my homework. ✓

_____

0 I <u>do</u> a shower every morning. ✗
have

1 I'm tired. Let's <u>take</u> a break now. ☐

_____

2 We just <u>went</u> the shopping for the party. ☐

_____

3 Try not to <u>do</u> a lot of mistakes. ☐

_____

4 Please don't <u>make</u> too much noise when you come back. ☐

_____

5 We <u>made</u> some great photos on holiday. ☐

_____

6 Did you <u>do</u> a good time at the party? ☐

_____

2 ★★☆ **Complete the sentences with the correct verb in the correct form.**

0 They _____*went*_____ skiing last winter.

1 I always _____ excited the day before my birthday.

2 I always _____ something at the weekend. I never stay at home.

3 We live near an airport – the planes _____ a lot of noise every day.

4 Our weekend was fantastic! We _____ a party at our house.

5 Every day, when I wake up, I _____ a bath.

6 We weren't hungry so we didn't _____ breakfast.

7 _____ you always _____ the train to school?

Adjectives

→ SB p.107

3 ★★☆ **Put the letters in order to make adjectives. Then look at the pictures and write the phrases.**

ovllye	ercvel	tydri	putdis	regnoudas	blehirro	gluy	teulauibf	tersniginet	lance

0 *a lovely gorilla* **1** _____ **2** _____ **3** _____ **4** _____ **5** _____ **6** _____ **7** _____ **8** _____ **9** _____

4 ★★☆ **Complete the crossword and the sentences with the same words. What's the mystery word?**

```
1 . . . . G
2 C . . .
3 . N . . . .
4 . L .
5 . I . .
6 . T . . . . . .
7 S . .
8 . P .
9 . . . Y
```

1 I don't like this film, it's really _____ .

2 Cats are very _____ animals.

3 Snakes can sometimes be _____ .

4 I don't like that house. I think it's _____ .

5 I have to wash my parents' car because it's very _____ .

6 The lesson today was great. It was really _____ .

7 Some big cities aren't very _____ at night.

8 Hey! That was a really _____ thing to do!

9 Thank you for my _____ birthday present.

Mystery word: _____

REFERENCE

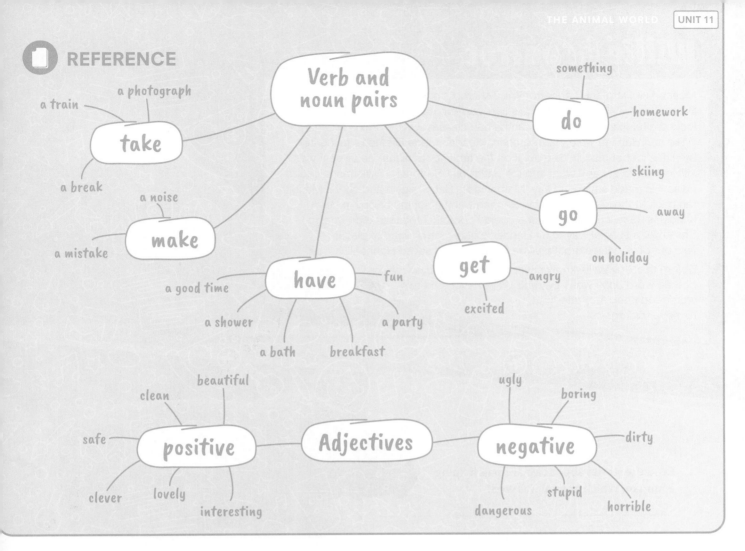

Verb and noun pairs

take — a train, a photograph, a break

make — a noise, a mistake

have — a good time, a shower, a bath, breakfast, fun, a party

get — angry, excited

go — skiing, away, on holiday

do — something, homework

Adjectives

positive — clean, beautiful, safe, clever, lovely, interesting

negative — ugly, boring, dirty, stupid, horrible, dangerous

VOCABULARY *EXTRA*

1 **Match the verb–noun combinations from the list with the definitions.**

> do nothing | get upset | go fishing
> go to bed | have dinner | make friends

0 lie down to sleep _____go to bed_____

1 meet new people to hang out with _____

2 feel bad about something, like losing your phone _____

3 activity in a river or the sea _____

4 eat in the evening _____

5 you sit in your room or on the sofa and relax _____

2 **Complete the sentences using the past form of the verbs and nouns in Exercise 1.**

0 At Ali's new school everyone was friendly and he _____made friends_____ quickly.

1 Yesterday I had a lot of homework and I _____ at midnight!

2 Yesterday they _____ at the new Italian restaurant.

3 Last Sunday we stayed at home and _____ all day. It was really boring.

4 My mum and I _____ today. We caught lots to eat for dinner.

5 My parents _____ because my sister lost her free bus pass again.

Willie the parrot

Meagan Howard and her parrot Willie shared a house in Colorado with Samantha Kuusk and Samantha's two-year-old daughter, Hannah. Meagan looked after Hannah when Samantha had classes. One morning Meagan, Willie and Hannah were in the kitchen. Meagan made Hannah's favourite breakfast, a hot biscuit. She put it on the table for a minute because it was still too hot to eat and went into the bathroom. Suddenly, Willie made a loud noise. He made sounds to say 'Mama!' and 'Baby!' again and again. Meagan ran back to the kitchen and saw Hannah with half of the biscuit in her hand. Her face was blue and she couldn't breathe! Meagan didn't panic. She knew a special way to hit Hannah's back and a piece of biscuit flew out of Hannah's mouth. Willie (and Meagan) saved Hannah!

Before that day Willie knew several words, including *mama*, but the word *baby* was new, and Willie never said two words together. And after that, he never did again!

READING

1 **Read the stories about two animals helping a human. Which animal was wild?**

_____

2 **Read the sentences and <u>underline</u> the incorrect information. Then write correct sentences.**

Willie and the parrot

0 Willie was Meagan's <u>daughter</u>.
  Willie was Meagan's parrot.

1 Meagan gave Hannah the hot biscuit.

_____

2 Meagan was in the kitchen when Hannah ate the biscuit.

_____

3 Willie often said two words together.

_____

Robert and the bear

4 Robert went for a walk with his dog.

_____

5 He was worried when he saw the bears.

_____

6 The mountain lion didn't hurt Robert.

_____

7 The bear and the lion fought for a long time.

_____

3  **Read the stories again and answer the questions.**

1 How did the animals in the stories help the humans?

2 Which animal do you think was very clever? Why?

Robert and the bear

Robert Biggs lived in Paradise, California. He often went walking near the Sequoia National Forest. One day, he went to the Whiskey Flat Trail, a beautiful walk. Robert was alone, but he enjoyed the quiet. He loved seeing animals and birds on his walks. This time, he saw a family of black bears (a mother and two young cubs) drinking at a river. Robert knew the bears because he sometimes saw them on his walks. Bears in California don't usually attack humans. Robert wasn't worried. He watched the bears playing. Then, suddenly, a mountain lion jumped on his back, and bit his arm. Before Robert could fight the lion, the mother bear ran over and attacked it. An adult bear is very big and strong, and after 15 seconds, the mountain lion ran away. The bear looked Robert in the eye and walked back to her cubs. She saved Robert's life.

DEVELOPING *Writing*

A blog entry about my favourite animal

1 **INPUT** **Read the text. Why did Ria choose to write about pandas?**

MY **FAVOURITE** ANIMAL: **GIANT PANDAS**

My favourite animal is the giant panda. They live in mountain forests in south central China. They eat bamboo, and drink water from rivers. They are my favourite animals because they look so cool. They have thick black and white fur. Giant pandas are very big, but they aren't usually aggressive. That means they don't usually attack people or other animals. They are also very lazy!

In the 1960s, the Chinese government opened some panda reserves – places where pandas and the bamboo they eat are safe – because wild pandas were in danger. In these reserves, there are doctors and experts to look after baby pandas. Because of this work, there are now nearly 1,860 wild pandas in China. The WWF organisation (the World Wide Fund for Nature) has the panda as its symbol, because everyone thinks pandas are cute!

2 **ANALYSE** **Put the headings in the order you find this information in the text.**

- [ ] What pandas eat and drink
- [ ] What pandas look like
- [ ] Other interesting information
- [1] Where pandas live
- [ ] Why pandas are Rita's favourite animal

3 **Complete the sentences with *but* or *because*.**

1 Pandas are very big _____ they aren't aggressive.

2 WWF use a panda symbol _____ everyone all round the world thinks they're cute.

3 Experts help pandas with their babies _____ the pandas have problems.

4 Pandas were in danger _____ now they aren't.

5 Some pandas get ill _____ doctors can usually help them.

6 I like pandas _____ they look very happy.

4 **PLAN** **Decide which animal is your favourite. Then read the questions and make notes about your animal for a blog post.**

- What is your favourite animal?
- Where does it live?
- What does it eat and drink?
- What does it look like?
- Why is it your favourite animal?
- What other interesting information can you think of about it?

 WRITING TIP: Using a model text

Before you write your own text, read the model text and look for any useful words or phrases you can use.

- *My favourite animal is the …*
- *They are my favourite animals because they …*

5 **PRODUCE** **Use your notes and the text from Exercise 1 and write a blog post about your favourite animal. Write about 80 words.**

🎧 LISTENING

1 🔊 **11.02** **Listen to Holly talking about volunteering at an animal rescue centre. Tick (✓) the animals that she talks about.**

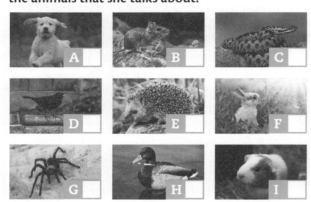

2 🔊 **11.02** **Listen again. Mark the sentences T (true) or F (false).**

0 The boy writes for the school website. [T]

1 Holly volunteers at the Rescue Centre after school. ☐

2 She couldn't work at the centre when she was 14. ☐

3 They get lots of different pets at the centre. ☐

4 Holly liked all the jobs she did at the centre. ☐

5 The police found the snake in the police station. ☐

6 Holly loves all animals. ☐

7 Holly wants to work in a zoo when she leaves school. ☐

8 There are some wild animals at the centre. ☐

DIALOGUE

3 **Complete the conversation with words and phrases from the list.**

> after that | and | because
> ~~but~~ | Poor you | Then

Adriana Did you have a good weekend?

Paulo Yes it was great, thanks. I went to Miguel's party.

Adriana Oh, right. He invited me, too, ⁰___*but*___ I couldn't go.

Paulo Why not?

Adriana My aunt and uncle were here for the weekend ¹_____ they wanted to take us out.

Paulo That's nice. Where did you go?

Adriana We went to the theatre. It was really boring.

Paulo ²_____ !

Adriana But ³_____ we went and had pizza. That was good! ⁴_____ I ordered an enormous ice cream. I couldn't eat it all, I was so full.

Paulo That's like me at the party. I couldn't dance ⁵_____ I was really tired from football on Saturday!

4 **Read the conversation again and answer the questions.**

1 Why couldn't Adriana go to the party?

_____

2 Why couldn't Adriana eat all the ice cream?

_____

3 Why couldn't Paulo dance at the party?

_____

PHRASES FOR FLUENCY → SB p.108

5 **Put the letters in order to make expressions.**

0 dunylsed ...   _____*suddenly ...*_____

1 lal thrig.   _____

2 opor oyu!   _____

3 thwa phedapen?   _____

6 **Complete the conversation with the expressions in Exercise 1.**

Eva Do you know what happened to me last weekend?

Katya No, of course not. I wasn't with you last weekend. ⁰ _*What happened?*_

Eva ¹_____ , I'll tell you. On Saturday, I was in the café in the High Street, and ²_____ someone waved at me!

Katya So? Who was it?

Eva It was Jenny Hall.

Katya Jenny Hall? Are you sure? Jenny's in the US! She moved last year.

Eva Well, she's here on holiday. But it was awful.

Katya Why?

Eva I couldn't remember her name! I called her Annie. And she got really angry with me! She shouted at me!

Katya Oh, ³_____ . I'm sure that was horrible for you!

BACK-IN-TIME TRAVEL

Welcome to the wonderful world of Back-in-Time Travel.

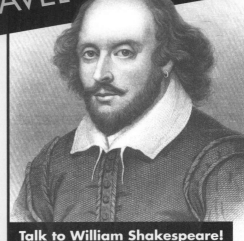

Talk to William Shakespeare!

As you know, last year the famous Professor Reddy of Bangalore University invented the **Back-in-Time Travel Machine**.

Now, you can go into the past! (Sorry, no future travel yet – maybe next year?)

Sit in the Back-in-Time, choose your time in the past – and whoosh! Off you go!

We are offering one-day trips to the past for only US$1,000,000! That's right! Only a million dollars for 24 hours in a past time period that you choose.

But here's some really good news – we have a competition and the five winners will get a free one-day trip in the Back-in-Time!

All you have to do is write to say what time in the past you want to travel to, and why. Write between 10 and 20 words, beginning with 'I want to go to …' Here are two examples to help you:

'I want to go to pre-history and see the dinosaurs because they're fantastic animals!' (Frieda, Germany)

'I want to go to 2006 because that's when my country won the World Cup, but I wasn't alive then!' (Bruno, Italy)

But remember – if you win, you must go to the time you wrote about!

Send your ideas to us at: Back-in-Time Travel, P.O. Box 2020, London

See the dinosaurs!

Watch the Egyptians building the pyramids!

1 Read the advertisement. Mark the sentences T (true) or F (false).

1 A man in New York invented the travel machine. ☐
2 You can travel to the past and into the future. ☐
3 You can buy a trip into the past for one million US dollars. ☐
4 The time trips are for one day. ☐
5 Five people can win a prize in the competition. ☐
6 If you win, you can go to any past time that you want. ☐

2 Imagine there's a time machine. Where would you like to go? Write an entry for the competition.

- Say what time in the past you want to travel to, and why.
- Write a paragraph, beginning with 'I want to go to …'

12 MOVING ABOUT

▶35 Grammar rap!

GRAMMAR
Comparative adjectives
 → SB p.112

1 ★☆☆ **Underline the comparative adjective in each sentence.**

0 The train is <u>quicker</u> than the car.
1 His bicycle is more expensive than my bicycle.
2 Surfing is more dangerous than tennis.
3 The weather in winter is worse than in summer.
4 Spanish is easier than Chinese.
5 Your phone is better than my phone.
6 My house is further from school than your house.
7 Their car is bigger than our car.
8 Salad is healthier than chips.

2 ★☆☆ **Complete the table with the correct adjective forms.**

adjective	comparative
0 dirty	*dirtier*
1 beautiful	
2 cold	
3	curlier
4 hot	
5	cleaner
6	shorter
7 ugly	
8	more boring
9 sad	
10 warm	
11 lovely	
12	slower
13	more interesting

3 ★★☆ **Look at the table and mark the sentences T (true) or F (false). Correct the false sentences.**

	Leaves Edinburgh	Arrives London	Price
train	8 am	1 pm	£140
bus	5 am	5 pm	£35
plane	10 am	11.30 am	£75

0 The train is cheaper than the bus. ☐ F
   The train is more expensive than the bus.
1 The bus arrives later than the train. ☐
   _____
2 The bus is slower than the plane. ☐
   _____
3 The bus is more expensive than the plane. ☐
   _____
4 The plane is faster than the train. ☐
   _____
5 The plane arrives earlier than the bus. ☐
   _____

4 ★★★ **Use the table in Exercise 3 to write sentences. Use comparative adjectives.**

0 bus / early / train
   The bus leaves earlier than the train.
1 train / fast / bus
   _____
2 plane / expensive / bus
   _____
3 train / slow / plane
   _____
4 bus / late / plane
   _____
5 bus / cheap / train
   _____

PRONUNCIATION
Word stress – comparatives
Go to page 121. 🎧

5 ★★★ Look at the pictures and write sentences to compare the two taxi companies. Use the adjectives in the list to help you.

> big | clean | dangerous | dirty
> expensive | fast | good | safe

0 *Lidia's limos are cleaner than Tim's taxis.*
1 _____
2 _____
3 _____
4 _____
5 _____
6 _____
7 _____

6 ★★★ Complete the sentences so they are true for you.

1 I'm _____ than my parents.
2 My best friend is _____ than me.
3 English lessons are _____ than Maths lessons.
4 Parrots are _____ than cats.
5 Summer is _____ than winter.
6 Walking is _____ than cycling.

one / ones   → SB p.115

7 ★☆☆ Circle the correct options.

0 Can I have a look at those jeans? The *one /(ones)* in the window.
1 Don't buy me a coffee. I don't want *one / ones*.
2 I like most films, but I don't like *one / ones* about war.
3 I can't give you a piece of paper because I haven't got *one / ones*.
4 I've got some apples. Would you like *one / ones*?
5 I'm interested in cars and I really like Italian *one / ones*.

8 ★★☆ Write *one* into the dialogues in the correct place.

0 A Where's your house?
  B My house is the first ^*one* on the left.

1 A How was your birthday?
  B Great. I got lots of presents, but my favourite was a book from my dad.

2 A Which dress did you buy?
  B Well, I love red, so I bought the red.

3 A How is your new computer?
  B It's faster than my old and it's easier to use.

4 A Is that your cousin over there?
  B Yes, he's the with the glasses.

GET IT RIGHT!

one and ones

We use *one* or *ones* after an adjective when we want to avoid repeating a noun.

✓ I like this song, it's a good one.
✗ I like this song, it's a good song.
✓ I wore my new shoes – the red ones.
✗ I wore my new shoes – the red shoes.

Replace one of the nouns with *one* or *ones*.

0 How much are the cakes? I mean the big cakes.
  How much are the cakes? I mean the big ones.
1 These tickets are expensive. We can find cheaper tickets.
  _____
2 This pen isn't good. I've got a better pen in my bag.
  _____
3 The blue jeans are too big. The black jeans are much better.
  _____
4 All of the buses go there but the red bus is the fastest.
  _____
5 Where are my black shoes? They were next to my brown shoes.
  _____

VOCABULARY
Transport

→ SB p.112

1 ★☆☆ **Find and circle five more types of transport in the word snake.**

agemotorbikeasehelicopternmbdplanerkutaxilfqferryipatrainbgh

2 ★★☆ **Put the letters in order to make the column titles. Then complete the table with words from Exercise 1.**

no het ardo 0 _on the road_	no sairl 1 _____	ni eth ria 2 _____	no tware 3 _____
motorbike			

3 ★★★ **Match the words from Exercise 1 with their definitions.**

0 It flies in the air, but it doesn't have wings.　_helicopter_

1 It travels on rails and is very long.　_____

2 It flies in the air. It has wings.　_____

3 It travels on water and carries a lot of people.　_____

4 You pay someone to drive you.　_____

5 It drives on the road, but only has two wheels.　_____

Geographical places

→ SB p.115

4 ★★☆ **Find the places in the word search. Write the words under the pictures.**

Q	H	C	A	E	B	W	W	M
H	E	E	O	F	G	S	O	S
F	V	S	U	D	R	U	E	E
O	M	C	D	U	N	A	K	R
R	H	R	R	T	B	A	E	U
E	T	P	A	B	L	V	S	C
S	X	I	E	F	I	P	B	T
T	N	C	K	R	R	T	D	B
Z	D	L	E	I	F	L	O	V

5 ★★☆ **Match the geographical places with the famous examples.**

1 mountain ☐

2 lake ☐

3 river ☐

4 beach ☐

5 sea ☐

a The Nile, The Amazon, The Yangtze

b Aconcagua, K2, Kilimanjaro

c Copacabana, Bondi, Kuta

d Caspian, Mediterranean, Red

e Michigan, Titicaca, Victoria

6 ★★★ **Complete the sentences with examples from your own country.**

1 My favourite beach is _____ .

2 The highest mountain is _____ .

3 A famous lake is _____ .

4 The longest river is _____ .

5 _____ is a good place to go on holiday.

6 _____ is a beautiful place in the winter.

forest

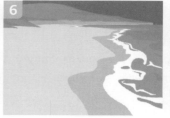

REFERENCE

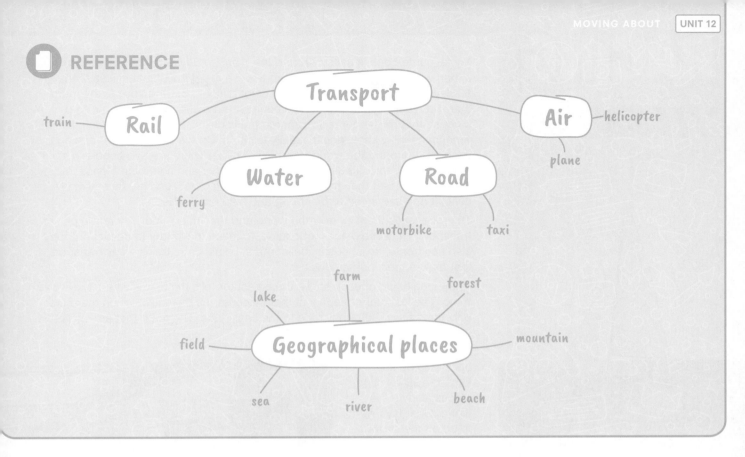

Transport
- Rail — train
- Water — ferry
- Road — motorbike, taxi
- Air — helicopter, plane

Geographical places — farm, lake, field, forest, mountain, sea, river, beach

VOCABULARY EXTRA

1 Label the pictures of day and night with the words from the list.

cloud | moon | sky | star | sun

1 _____

2 _____

3 _____

4 _____

5 _____

2 Choose the correct answers (A, B or C).

1 The colour of the sky is really _____ .

  A blue   B red   C no colour

2 The sun is _____ million kilometres from our planet.

  A 98.7   B 149.6   C 203.5

3 A cloud is _____ .

  A air with water or ice in it   B hot   C water or ice

4 The moon goes around the earth every _____ .

  A 30.25 days   B 29.98 days   C 27.32 days

5 There are about _____ stars in the universe.

  A 1 billion   B 1 trillion   C 1 billion trillion

Answers: 1 A – We see blue light because of air molecules; 2 B; 3 A; 4 C; 5 C (very approximately)

RACING AROUND THE WORLD!

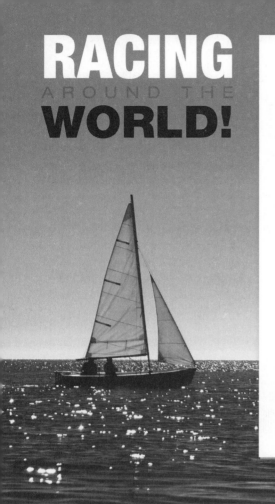

My favourite book is called *Around the World in 80 Days*. It's the story of a man who makes a bet that he can travel around the planet in less than 80 days. Of course, these days that's not difficult, but the book is set more than 100 years ago. I love the idea of adventure and exploring, so it's no surprise that my favourite TV programme is called *The Amazing Race*. It's an American reality show and it's really exciting. On the show, teams race against each other around the world to win a big prize. There are two people in each team, for example, a husband and wife, a father and son, best friends, etc. It's important that they have a good relationship because the race is really difficult and they need to be strong and help each other.

The race takes them all over the world and they use lots of different types of transport. They use planes, of course, to make the longer journeys, but they also use boats, taxis, buses, helicopters, bikes, cars, trains – any transport that makes their journey quicker.

At the beginning of each show, the presenter tells the teams where they have to go. The last team to arrive at that place leaves the show. When there are only three teams left, they race to the final place. The team that arrives first usually wins lots of money.

I love this show because you see lots of really exciting places all over the world. One day I want to be on the show.

📖 READING

1   **Read the blog. Which of these types of transport is <u>not</u> mentioned?**

2   **Read the blog again and match the sentence halves.**

0	*Around the World in 80 Days*	g
1	*The Amazing Race*	☐
2	The race is	☐
3	The people in the teams	☐
4	The teams race	☐
5	The teams use	☐
6	The last team to arrive	☐
7	In the final	☐
8	The winning team	☐

a   between teams of two people.
b   all over the world.
c   leaves the show.
d   gets lots of money.
e   is a TV show from the US.
f   lots of different types of transport.
g   is a famous book.
h   know each other.
i   there are three teams.

3   CRITICAL THINKING **Do you want to be on *The Amazing Race*? Why/Why not? Write a short paragraph (60–80 words).**

DEVELOPING Writing

Writing about a journey

1 **INPUT** **Read about Eric and Alexia's favourite journeys. Do they prefer leaving or coming home?**

Eric

My favourite journey is the one I make every Saturday morning to play basketball. I leave my house at about nine o'clock and get on my bike to cycle the three kilometres to the sports club. It takes me about 15 minutes. At the club, I meet my team and we play a game. Then I get on my bike and ride back home. I like the journey there because I get excited about playing basketball. I don't like the journey back so much because I'm usually quite tired. But when I have a good game, the journey back is great, too, because I think about the game.

Alexia

The journey I like best is the one from my house to my dad's house. My dad lives in Greece and three times every year I fly there to spend some time with him. The journey starts really early. The taxi picks me up from my house at 4 am! But that's OK, because I'm always really happy. It's only 30 minutes to the airport, but I can't wait to get there. The plane journey is about four hours. It's not very exciting, but I usually listen to music or go to sleep. My dad always meets me at the airport and then he drives me to his house. We don't stop talking the whole journey. I never like the journey back. I'm always really sad to leave.

2 **ANALYSE** **Read the texts again and complete the table.**

	from	to	transport	time it takes	why I like it
Eric					
Alexia					

3 **PLAN** **Think about your favourite journey and make notes to complete the table so it is true for you.**

	from	to	transport	time	why I like it
Me					

4 **PRODUCE** **Use your notes to write a text about your favourite journey. Write 35–50 words.**

✎ WRITING TIP: Useful language

- *My favourite journey is the one I make* (every Saturday morning) *to* (play basketball).
- *The journey I like best is the one from* (my house) *to* (my dad's house).
- *The journey starts* (really early).
- *It takes me about* (15 minutes).
- *I like the journey there because* (I get excited about playing basketball.)
- *I don't like the journey back* (so much) *because* (I'm usually quite tired).

1 🔊 12.02 **Listen to the conversation. Where is Jill? Who is she talking to?**

_____

2 🔊 12.02 **Listen again and (circle) the correct answers (A, B or C).**

0 Where does Jill want to go?
   A Central London
   Ⓑ Liverpool
   C Manchester

1 What time is the next train?
   A
   B
   C

2 How often is there a train?
   A every 15 minutes
   B every 30 minutes
   C every 50 minutes

3 How long is the journey?
   A 40 minutes
   B 35 minutes
   C 45 minutes

4 When is Jill returning?
   A today
   B tomorrow
   C at the weekend

5 How much is the ticket?
   A £7.80
   B £8.70
   C £17.80

6 What platform is the train leaving from?
   A 3
   B 4
   C 5

7 What time does Jill get the train?
   A
   B
   C

DIALOGUE

3 **(Circle) the correct options. Then put the conversation in order.**

	Assistant	The journey is three ¹*quarters* / *halves* of an hour.
	Assistant	OK, that's £5.50, please.
	Assistant	Platform 5. Have a ²*good* / *boring* journey.
	Assistant	Let me see. There's a train every 15 minutes so the next one is at half past three.
	Assistant	Do you want a single or a return?
1	Assistant	Good afternoon. ³*How* / *Who* can I help you?
	Woman	That's great. And how long does it take?
	Woman	Thank you.
	Woman	I want to ⁴*go* / *come* to Liverpool. What time's the next train?
	Woman	Just one more thing. What platform does the train leave ⁵*from* / *at*?
	Woman	45 minutes. That's quick. Can I have a ticket, please?
	Woman	Return, please. I'm coming back later.

Train to TH!NK

Comparing

4 **Complete the diagram with the words from the list. Then use your own ideas and write six more words.**

> boring | dangerous | exciting
> expensive | fun | relaxing

Holidays by the sea

Holidays in the mountains

5 **Write sentences to compare the two different types of holidays in Exercise 4.**

_____

_____

_____

TOWARDS A2 Key for Schools

EXAM SKILLS: READING
Answering open cloze questions

1 **Read Matteo's answers in the task below. How many did he get right? How many did he get wrong?**

Complete the text about travelling to and from school. Write ONE word for each space.

I live ⁰_____*in*_____ a small town and my school is about six kilometres away. Most days I take the school bus. It stops outside my house ¹_____*at*_____ 7.30 every morning. In the summer, when the weather ²_____*are*_____ good, I usually cycle to school. It's quicker ³_____*than*_____ the bus because the bus stops all the time. The problem with the bike is when my school bag is too heavy. Then it's ⁴_____*not*_____ fun. Sometimes I wake up late and ⁵_____*mis*_____ the school bus. Mum takes me to school ⁶_____*in*_____ the car. She doesn't like this ⁷_____*because*_____ she needs to get to work, too. Once I missed the bus home and I had to ⁸_____*tired*_____ home. It took me more than ⁹_____*half an*_____ hour to walk. I don't want ¹⁰_____*to*_____ do that again.

READING TIP:

- Read the instructions carefully. Underline the key words. Words like *circle*, *tick*, *choose* and *underline* tell you how to complete the question. Look for other important information, for example, *Write ONE word for each space.*
- When you have finished, read your answers again. Have you followed the instructions? Have you used the correct type of word (verb, noun, adjective, etc.)? Have you used the singular and plural forms correctly? Is your spelling correct?
- Don't leave any gaps. If you don't know the answer, guess!

2 **Put Matteo's mistakes under the correct heading. Write the number.**

Used more than one word	Used the wrong type of word (adjective instead of verb)	Used singular and plural forms incorrectly	Used incorrect spelling
9			

3 **Correct Matteo's mistakes. Write the correct words next to the numbers in Exercise 2.**

4 **Complete the text about favourite holidays. Write ONE word for each space.**

My favourite holidays ⁰_____*are*_____ beach holidays. I like the sun ¹_____ the sea. I usually go on beach holidays ²_____ the summer with my family. Sometimes Dad drives and sometimes we ³_____ the train. Last year, we went ⁴_____ holiday in the countryside. We stayed on ⁵_____ farm. There was a river and a lake and lots ⁶_____ fields, too. It was OK, but I prefer beach holidays. The weather by the sea is usually hotter ⁷_____ in the countryside. Dad wants to ⁸_____ on holiday in the mountains this year. I'm ⁹_____ happy about that idea. I don't want another year away ¹⁰_____ the beach.

CONSOLIDATION

🎧 LISTENING

1   🔊 12.03   **Listen to Arnau and circle the correct answers (A, B or C).**

  1 How old is Arnau's brother?
    A eight   B nine   C ten

  2 At the zoo, which animals scared Arnau's brother?
    A the elephants   B the lions   C the tigers

  3 How many jaguars were there?
    A two   B three   C four

2   🔊 12.03   **Listen again and answer the questions.**

  1 Why did Arnau's family go to the zoo?
    _____

  2 Who took photos at the zoo?
    _____

  3 What was Arnau happy about?
    _____

  4 What did Arnau think about the visit to the zoo?
    _____

  5 Why was Arnau sorry for the jaguars?
    _____

  6 What two things does Arnau think zoo animals need?
    _____

Ⓖ GRAMMAR

3   **Complete the sentences with the correct form of the words in brackets.**

  1 Yesterday I _____ some money in the street in town. (find)

  2 For my last birthday, my parents _____ me tickets for a concert. (give)

  3 My friends and I _____ to the cinema three times last month. (go)

  4 I arrived home late last night, but I _____ any noise. (not make)

  5 Yesterday's test was _____ than the one on Friday. (difficult)

  6 _____ you _____ that film on TV last Sunday night? (see)

  7 The weather today is _____ than yesterday. (bad)

  8 I practise a lot and I'm getting _____ every day! (good)

  9 I _____ many presents for my birthday. (not get)

  10 Are tigers _____ than jaguars? (big)

🅰️ VOCABULARY

4   **Circle the odd one out in each list. Explain your reasons.**

  0 safe   clean   (homework)
    It's a noun – the other two are adjectives.

  1 motorbike   plane   helicopter
    _____

  2 shopping   homework   a mistake
    _____

  3 forest   sea   lake
    _____

  4 train   river   underground
    _____

  5 a break   a good time   photos
    _____

  6 boat   ferry   taxi
    _____

  7 a mistake   a shower   a noise
    _____

  8 breakfast   elephant   horse
    _____

  9 field   beach   farm
    _____

5   **Use a word or phrase from Exercise 4 to complete each sentence.**

  1 Shh! Don't make _____ or that pretty bird will fly away.

  2 We went for a walk in the _____ this morning. The trees were very beautiful.

  3 My mum doesn't like me riding my bike in the city. She thinks it isn't _____ .

  4 This party's great. I'm having _____ .

  5 Her name's Julie but I made _____ and called her Jenny.

  6 I like having _____ after football to get clean again!

  7 We went to the beach, but I didn't swim in the _____ – I think it's dangerous.

  8 I'm really tired. Let's take _____ and have some coffee.

DIALOGUE

6 🔊 **12.04** Complete the dialogue with the words and phrases from the list. There are two extra words/phrases. Then listen and check.

> All right | better | came | cheaper | could | didn't | Did | lovely | made | Poor you | suddenly | What happened

Jin How was your weekend at the beach?

Maria Oh, awful. Everything went wrong.

Jin Oh, dear. ¹_____ ?

Maria Well, first, we missed the train.

Jin But you got there in the end?

Maria Oh, yes, we got there. We always stay at the same hotel. But it's very expensive, so this year Dad said: 'Let's stay at a ²_____ hotel.' I said, 'Dad! If our usual hotel is more expensive, that's because it's ³_____ than the cheaper ones.' ⁴_____ he listen? No, he didn't. The hotel was horrible! I ⁵_____ sleep at all – there were cars outside all night. They ⁶_____ a lot of noise!

Jin ⁷_____ , but what about the beach?

Maria The beach there is really ⁸_____ . We like it a lot. So we went there on the first day – but ⁹_____ it started to rain! We ¹⁰_____ home a day early. The weekend was … well, it was horrible.

📖 READING

The Scottish Highlands — there's nowhere more beautiful!

Are you thinking about taking a break? Then try the Scottish Highlands. This lovely part of Scotland has forests, rivers, lakes – called *lochs* in Scotland – and, of course, mountains! The mountains are beautiful and quiet, with fantastic walks. Check the weather first, though, as it can change very quickly!

The town of Inverness is the capital of the Highlands. It has lots of interesting shops and restaurants. Try haggis, a Scottish speciality. You can also visit Cawdor Castle, 14 miles away. Inverness is on the coast, so there's a beach, but it can be cold, even in the summer!

Another place to see is Loch Ness, the lake famous for its monster, Nessie! Visit the museum or take a boat trip across the loch.

There are lots of hotels and bed-and-breakfast places in the Highlands. The B&Bs are cheaper, but sometimes they're as good as hotels. The breakfasts are really big, so expect to be full all day! They often serve afternoon tea, with sandwiches and cakes, too.

You can get to Inverness or Fort William by train, but to visit the lochs and the mountains, it's easier to drive. Why not visit the Highlands soon? We'd love to see you!

7 Read the web page. Mark the sentences T (true) or F (false).

1 Lakes in Scotland have a different name. ☐
2 You have to check the weather before you go for a walk. ☐
3 There isn't a lot to do in Inverness. ☐
4 Loch Ness has a famous monster. ☐
5 B&Bs are more expensive than hotels. ☐
6 At the B&B places, you usually get a small breakfast. ☐
7 You can't visit everywhere in the Highlands by train. A car is better. ☐

✏️ WRITING

8 Write a paragraph about a nice area that you know. Write 60–80 words. Use the questions to help you.

- What is it called?
- What are the good things about it?
- What can people do there?
- How can you get there?

PRONUNCIATION

UNIT 1
/h/ or /w/ in question words

1 **Look at the question words. Two of them start with the /h/ sound and the others start with the /w/ sound. Write /h/ or /w/ next to the words.**

   0 Why _____/w/_____
   1 How _____
   2 Where _____
   3 Who _____
   4 What _____
   5 When _____

2 🔊 1.01 **Listen, check and repeat.**

3 **Match the words that sound the same.**

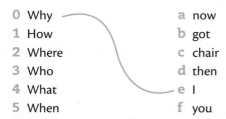

   0 Why   a now
   1 How   b got
   2 Where   c chair
   3 Who   d then
   4 What   e I
   5 When   f you

4 🔊 1.02 **Listen, check and repeat.**

UNIT 2
Vowel sounds – adjectives

1 🔊 2.01 **Listen and repeat the adjectives.**

a<u>ng</u>ry	<u>aw</u>ful	b<u>o</u>red	b<u>u</u>sy
fr<u>ie</u>ndly	f<u>u</u>nny	h<u>a</u>ppy	h<u>o</u>t
h<u>u</u>ngry	s<u>a</u>d	th<u>ir</u>sty	w<u>o</u>rried

2 **Complete the table with the words in Exercise 1.**

a (c<u>a</u>t)	e (g<u>e</u>t)	i (s<u>i</u>x)	o (d<u>o</u>g)
0 angry	3 _____	4 _____	5 _____
1 _____			
2 _____			

u (b<u>u</u>s)	or (f<u>or</u>)	ir (b<u>ir</u>d)	
6 _____	9 _____	11 _____	
7 _____	10 _____		
8 _____			

3 🔊 2.02 **Listen, check and repeat.**

UNIT 3
this / that / these / those

1 🔊 3.01 **Listen and repeat. Then look at the underlined sounds and ⟲circle the odd sound out.**

0	th<u>o</u>se	<u>g</u>o	h<u>o</u>me	⟲b<u>o</u>red⟳
1	<u>th</u>at	sa<u>d</u>	la<u>t</u>e	ha<u>v</u>e
2	th<u>e</u>m	th<u>e</u>se	pl<u>ea</u>se	m<u>ee</u>t
3	<u>g</u>ive	li<u>k</u>e	thi<u>s</u>	sin<u>g</u>
4	h<u>o</u>t	c<u>o</u>ld	kn<u>o</u>w	th<u>o</u>se
5	w<u>i</u>fe	th<u>i</u>s	n<u>i</u>ce	exc<u>i</u>ting
6	<u>th</u>ese	<u>sh</u>e	ge<u>t</u>	w<u>e</u>
7	f<u>a</u>mous	<u>th</u>at	f<u>a</u>mily	h<u>a</u>ppy

2 🔊 3.02 **Listen again, check and repeat.**

UNIT 4
Word stress in numbers

1 🔊 **4.01** **Listen to the words and write them in the correct column according to the stress.**

> eighteen | eighty | forty | fourteen | nineteen
> ninety | sixteen | sixty | thirty | thirteen

oO	Oo
eighteen	eighty

2 🔊 **4.01** **Listen again, check and repeat.**

UNIT 5
Present simple verbs – third person

1 **Complete the table with the correct present simple third person singular form of the verbs in the list.**

> catch | cook | choose | dance | help | look
> sing | teach | walk | wash | watch | wish | work

one syllable	two syllables
cooks	catches

2 🔊 **5.01** **Listen, check and repeat.**

UNIT 6
Long vowel sound /eɪ/

1 🔊 **6.01** **Listen to these words. They all contain the /eɪ/ sound. Underline the sound in each word.**

0	br<u>ea</u>k
1	eight
2	face
3	great
4	grey
5	make
6	rainy
7	say
8	straight
9	take
10	they
11	waiter

2 **Complete the sentences with the words in Exercise 1.**

0 How do you _____say_____ that word in English?
1 Is your grandmother the woman with the wavy _____ hair?
2 Let's _____ Clara a friendship band for her birthday!
3 My little sister is _____ years old.
4 These are my friends. _____ like playing football with me.
5 It's _____ today. Let's go to the cinema.
6 My father's a _____ at that restaurant.
7 I brush my teeth and wash my _____ every morning.
8 I like playing tennis. It's a _____ game!
9 Can you _____ this book to your teacher? Thank you.
10 My hair's _____ , but my best friend's hair is curly.
11 Put your books away. It's time for a _____ .

3 🔊 **6.02** **Listen, check and repeat.**

UNIT 7
Long vowel sound /ɔː/

1 🔊 7.01 **Listen to these words. They all contain the /ɔː/ sound. Underline the sound in each word.**

0	<u>Au</u>gust
1	autumn
2	daughter
3	door
4	forty
5	important
6	quarter
7	short
8	snowboarding
9	sport
10	walk
11	water

2 **Complete the sentences with the words in Exercise 1.**

0 Please close the ____door____ when you go out.
1 It's a beautiful day. Let's go for a _____ .
2 In _____ the leaves change to orange and it gets colder.
3 English is a very _____ language.
4 My birthday's on the fourth of _____ .
5 The tall girl with the curly hair is my teacher's _____ .
6 Jenny likes _____ in the mountains in winter.
7 My favourite _____ is volleyball.
8 I'm thirsty. Can I have a glass of _____ , please?
9 My hair is long, but my friend's is _____ .
10 My first class at school starts at _____ to nine in the morning.
11 It's my father's birthday today. He's _____ years old.

3 🔊 7.02 **Listen, check and repeat.**

UNIT 8
Intonation – listing items

1 **Complete the lists. Then draw a ↗ and a ↘ to show where intonation rises and falls in each list.**

> arm | Brazil | catch | coat | cooker | headphones
> library | Russian | rugby | ~~June~~ | spring | wife

↗ ↗ ↗   ↘

0 March, April, May and ____*June*____

1 son, daughter, husband and _____

2 Japanese, British, _____ and Turkish

3 _____ , skirt, socks and trousers

4 snowboarding, gymnastics, golf and _____

5 summer, _____ , winter and autumn

6 watch, choose, throw and _____

7 _____ , shower, fridge and armchair

8 Australia, Scotland, _____ and Japan

9 body, _____ , leg and face

10 tablet, GPS, _____ and laptop

11 _____ , restaurant, museum and bank

2 🔊 8.01 **Listen, check and repeat.**

UNIT 9
Intonation – giving two choices

1 🔊 9.01 **Complete the dialogue with the words in the list. Then listen and check.**

> chicken | chips | fish | ice cream
> pineapple | ~~soup~~ | tea | water

↗   ↘

Waiter	Would you like salad or ⁰____soup____ ?
Woman	Salad, please.

☐   ☐

Waiter	Chicken or ¹_____ ?
Woman	I think I'll have ²_____ today – with ³_____ , please.
Waiter	Would you like dessert?
Woman	Yes, please.

☐   ☐

Waiter	Cake or ⁴_____ ?
Woman	I'd prefer fruit – some ⁵_____ , please.
Waiter	Would you like something to drink?
Woman	Yes, please – just some ⁶_____ . And a cup of ⁷_____ after the meal. Thank you.

2 🔊 9.01 **Draw ↗ or ↘ above the waiter's questions. Then listen, check and repeat.**

UNIT 10
Past simple regular verbs

1 **Say the verbs in the list in the past tense and decide if they are one syllable or two. Then write the verbs in the correct column.**

> ~~dance~~ | ~~hate~~ | help | like | live | need
> play | start | wait | walk | want | work

one syllable	two syllables
danced	hated

2 🔊 10.01 **Listen, check and repeat.**

3 **Complete the rule.**

We only say /ɪd/ when the final sound in the word is a / _____ / or a / _____ /.

UNIT 11
Short vowel sound /ʊ/

1 **Circle the odd sound out.**

0	(cook)	cool	food
1	house	shout	could
2	June	put	who
3	room	you	woods
4	pull	fun	son
5	foot	full	jump
6	move	zoo	good
7	funny	woolly	sunny
8	school	room	book
9	push	run	bus
10	cousin	couldn't	country

2 🔊 11.01 **Listen, check and repeat.**

UNIT 12
Word stress – comparatives

1 **Write the comparative form of the adjectives. Underline the stressed syllable.**

0	slow	_slower_	8	big	_____
1	small	_____	9	hot	_____
2	quick	_____	10	funny	_____
3	cheap	_____	11	easy	_____
4	fast	_____	12	healthy	_____
5	cold	_____	13	happy	_____
6	safe	_____	14	far	_____
7	close	_____	15	good	_____

2 🔊 12.01 **Listen, check and repeat.**

3 **Complete the rule.**

When adding *-er* to make a comparative, the *first / second* syllable is always stressed.

GRAMMAR REFERENCE

UNIT 1
Question words

1 **Questions that begin with *Who* ask about a person/people.**

   Who is he?
   He's the new teacher.

2 **Questions that begin with *What* ask about a thing/things.**

   What's that?
   It's a mobile phone.

3 **Questions that begin with *When* ask about a time/day/year, etc.**

   When's the football match?
   It's at three o'clock.

4 **Questions that begin with *Where* ask about a place.**

   Where's Cambridge?
   It's in the UK.

5 **Questions that begin with *Why* ask for a reason.**

   Why are you here?
   Because I want to see you.

6 **Questions that begin with *How old* ask about age.**

   How old is she?
   She's sixteen.

to be

1 **The present simple of *to be* is like this:**

Singular	Plural
I am	we are
you are	you are
he/she/it is	they are

2 **In speaking and informal writing we use contracted (short) forms.**

   I'm, you're, he's, she's, it's, we're, they're
   I'm from Russia.
   She's late.
   We're hungry.

UNIT 2
to be (negative, singular and plural)

1 **We make the verb *to be* negative by adding *not*.**

Singular	Plural
I am not (I'm not)	we are not (we aren't)
you are not (you aren't)	you are not (you aren't)
he/she/it is not (he/she/it isn't)	they are not (they aren't)

   I'm not Brazilian. I'm Portuguese.
   He isn't late. He's early!
   They aren't from Spain. They're from Mexico.

to be (questions and short answers)

To make questions with *to be*, we put the verb before the subject. We make short answers with *Yes* or *No* + subject + the verb *to be*. We don't use contracted forms in positive short answers (NOT: *Yes, you're.*)

Am I late?	Yes, you are. / No, you aren't.
Are you American?	Yes, I am. / No, I'm not.
Is he a singer?	Yes, he is. / No, he isn't.
Is she from Japan?	Yes, she is. / No, she isn't.
Are we right?	Yes, we are. / No, we aren't.
Are they French?	Yes, they are. / No, they aren't.

Object pronouns

1 **Object pronouns come after a verb. We use them instead of nouns.**

   I like the film. I like it.
   I love my sister. I love her.
   They are friends with you and me. They are friends with us.
   I like the girls at my school. I like them.

2 **The object pronouns are:**

Subject	I	you	he	she	it	we	they
Object	me	you	him	her	it	us	them

UNIT 3
Possessive 's

1 **We use 's after a noun to say who something belongs to.**

Dad's room
John's car
Sandra's family
the cat's bed
my brother's friend
your sister's school

2 **We don't usually say ~~the room of Dad, the car of John~~, etc.**

Possessive adjectives

1 **We use possessive adjectives before a noun to say who something belongs to.**

My name's Joanne.
Is this your pen?
He's my brother. I'm his sister.
She's nice. I like her smile!
The cat isn't on its bed.
We love our house.
Are the students in their classroom?

2 **The possessive adjectives are:**

Subject pronoun	I	you	he	she	it	we	they
Possessive adjective	my	your	his	her	its	our	their

this / that / these / those

1 **We use *this* or *these* to point out things that are close to us. We use *that* or *those* to point out things that are not close to us, or are close to other people.**

Look at this photograph – it's my sister.
These oranges aren't very nice.
That shop is a really good place for clothes.
We don't like those boys.

2 **We use *this* or *that* with a singular noun. We use *these* or *those* with plural nouns.**

this photo   *that house*
these rooms   *those tables*

UNIT 4
there is / there are

1 ***there is (there's)** and **there are** are used to say that something exists.*

There's a small shop in our street.
There are two supermarkets near here.
There are lots of great shops in the town centre.

2 ***there's** is the short form of **there is**. In speaking and informal writing, we usually say **there's**.*

3 **In positive sentences, we use *there's* with a singular noun and *there are* with plural nouns.**

There's a cat in the garden.
There's an old lady in the café.
There are nice shops in this street.

4 **In questions and negative sentences, we use *a/an* with a singular noun and *any* with plural nouns.**

Is there a bank near here?   *There isn't a bank near here.*
Are there any restaurants here?   *There aren't any restaurants here.*

some / any

1 **We use *some* and *any* with plural nouns.**

There are some good films on TV tonight.
There aren't any games on my tablet.

2 **We use *some* in positive sentences. We use *any* in negative sentences and questions.**

There are some nice trees in the park.
There aren't any places to play football here.
Are there any good shoe shops in the town?

Imperatives

1 **We use the imperative to tell someone to do something, or not to do something.**

Come here!
Don't open the door!

2 **The positive imperative is the same as the base form of the verb.**

Turn right.
Open the window, please.

3 **The negative imperative is formed with *Don't* and the base form of the verb.**

Don't listen to him – he's wrong!
Don't open the window – it's cold in here.

UNIT 5

Present simple

1 **The present simple is used to talk about things that happen regularly or are usually true.**

   I **go** to school at 8 o'clock every day.
   She **watches** TV after school.
   We **play** the piano.
   They **love** chocolate.

2 **The present simple is usually the same as the base form, but we add -s with third person singular (he/she/it).**

   I **like** pizza.   He **likes** pizza.
   They **live** in London.   She **lives** in London.

3 **If the verb ends with o, sh, ch, ss, z or x, we add -es.**

   go – he go**es**   finish – it finish**es**   catch – she catch**es**
   miss – it miss**es**   fix – he fix**es**

4 **If the verb ends with a consonant + -y, the y changes to i and we add -es.**

   carry – it carr**ies**   study – he stud**ies**   fly – it fl**ies**

5 **If the verb ends with a vowel + -y, it is regular.**

   buy – she buy**s**   say – he say**s**

Adverbs of frequency

1 **Adverbs of frequency tell us *how often* people do things. Adverbs of frequency include:**

   always   usually   often   sometimes   hardly ever   never

   ——————————————————————————→
   100%   0%

2 **Adverbs of frequency come after the verb *be*, but before other verbs.**

   I'm **always** hungry in the morning.
   I **usually have** breakfast at 7.00.
   He's **often** tired.   He **sometimes goes** to bed early.
   They're **never** late.   They **hardly ever** go on holiday.

Present simple (negative)

The present simple negative is formed with *don't* (do not) or *doesn't* (does not) + base form of the verb.

I **don't play** tennis.
She **doesn't play** football.
My grandparents **don't live** with us.
My brother **doesn't live** with us.

Present simple (questions)

Present simple questions are formed with *Do / Does* + subject + base form of the verb.

Do you like the film?   **Does Mike like** shopping?
Do I know you?   **Does she know** the answer?
Do your friends play video games?   **Does your dog play** with a ball?

UNIT 6

have / has got (positive and negative)

1 **The verb *have / has got* is used to talk about things that people own.**

   I've **got** a bicycle. (= There is a bicycle and it is my bicycle.)
   He's **got** a problem. (= There is a problem and it is his problem.)

2 **We use *have got* with I/you/we/they. We use *has got* with he/she/it. In speaking and informal writing, we often use the short forms: 've got / 's got.**

   My mother's **got** black hair and blue eyes.
   My friends **have got** a nice cat.
   We've **got** two fridges in our kitchen.

3 **The negative form is *hasn't / haven't got*.**

   I **haven't got** a tablet.
   This town **hasn't got** a park.
   They **haven't got** a car.

have / has got (questions)

We make questions with *Has/Have* + subject + got. Short answers use *has/have* or *hasn't/haven't*. Remember that we don't use contracted forms in positive short answers (e.g. NOT: Yes, ~~I've.~~)

Have you got my book?   Yes, I **have**.
Has your father got brown hair?   Yes, he **has**.
Has the shop got any new games?   No, it **hasn't**.

Countable and uncountable nouns

Nouns in English are countable or uncountable.

1 **Countable nouns have a singular and a plural form. We can count them. We use *a/an* with the singular nouns. We can use *some* with the plural nouns.**

   He's got **a house**.   He's got **two houses**.
   There's **a picture** on my wall.   There are **six pictures** on my wall.

   There's **an orange** in the fridge.   There are **some oranges** in the fridge.

2 **Uncountable nouns are always singular – they haven't got a plural form. We can't count them. We can use *some* with uncountable nouns.**

   I like **music**.   Let's listen to **some music**.
   I like Japanese **food**.   Let's eat **some** Japanese **food**.

3 **We don't use *a/an* or numbers with uncountable nouns.**

   NOT ~~a bread~~   ~~an information~~   ~~three works~~

UNIT 7
can (ability)

1 We use *can* / *can't* to talk about ability.

*I **can** swim.*
*I **can't** drive a car.*
*He **can** play the guitar.*
*He **can't** sing.*

2 The form is *can* / *can't* + the base form of the verb. To make questions, we use *Can* + subject + the base form of the verb. (We don't use *do* / *does* with *can* in questions or negative forms.)

*It's very small – I **can't** read it. (NOT: I don't can read it.)*
***Can you play** this game? (NOT: Do you can play this game?)*

3 Short answers are *Yes, … can* or *No, … can't.*

*Can he swim? **Yes, he can.***
*Can you sing? **No, I can't.***

Prepositions of time

We use different prepositions to talk about time.

1 With times of the day, we use *at.*

*School starts **at** eight o'clock.*
*The train leaves **at** seven thirty.*

2 With months and seasons, we use *in.*

*It always rains **in** December.*
*We play football **in** winter.*

3 With days of the week, we use *on.*

*I go to the cinema **on** Saturday.*
*There's a test at school **on** Monday.*

UNIT 8
Present continuous

1 We use the present continuous to talk about things that are happening at the moment of speaking.

*Please be quiet – I**'m watching** a film.*
*They're in the dining room – they**'re having** dinner.*
*Dad's in his office but he **isn't working**.*
*Hey, Alex – **are** you **listening** to me?*

2 We form the present continuous with the present simple of *be* + the *-ing* form of the main verb. Questions and negatives are formed with the question/negative form of *be* + the *-ing* form of the main verb.

*I**'m watching** a film but I**'m not enjoying** it.*
*They**'re playing** football but they **aren't playing** well.*
***Are** you **having** a good time? Yes, we **are**.*
***Is** she **doing** her homework? No, she **isn't**.*

3 If the verb ends in *-e*, we omit the *e* before adding *-ing*. If the verb ends in a consonant + vowel + consonant, we double the consonant before adding *-ing*.

leave   *We're **leaving** now.*
get   *It's **getting** dark – let's go home.*

like / don't like + -ing

When we use the verbs (*don't*) *like, love, hate* and another verb, we usually use the *-ing* form of the other verb.

*We **love living** here.*
*I **like dancing** at parties.*
*She **doesn't like listening** to classical music.*
*They **hate going** to the theatre.*

UNIT 9

must / mustn't

We use must / mustn't to talk about rules.

1 We use *must* to say that it's necessary to do something.

   *We **must leave** now.*
   *You **must go** to the doctor.*

2 We use *mustn't* to say that it's necessary not to do something.

   *You **mustn't tell** other people.*
   *We **mustn't be** late.*

3 The form is *must / mustn't* + the base form of the verb. We don't use *do / does* in negative sentences.

   *You must **ask** me first.*
   *I mustn't **eat** a lot of sweets before dinner.*
   (**NOT** ~~I don't must eat a lot of sweets before dinner.~~)

can (asking for permission)

1 We often use *Can I* + verb to ask for permission (ask if it's OK) to do something.

   ***Can I ask** a question, please?*
   ***Can I watch** the match on TV now?*

2 We use *can* or *can't* to give or refuse permission.

   ***Can I use** your phone?*   *Yes, you **can**.*
                                  *No, sorry, you **can't**. I'm using it.*

I'd like … / Would you like …?

1 We use *would ('d)* + *like* to ask for something, or to offer something, in a nice way. It is more polite than *want*.

   ***I'd like** a sandwich, please.*
   ***Would you like** a dessert?*

2 *I'd like* is the short form of *I would like*. We almost always use it in speaking and informal writing.

UNIT 10

Past simple: was / wasn't, were / weren't, there was / were

1 We use the past simple form of *to be* to talk about actions and events in the past.

   *It **was** a lovely day yesterday.*
   *They **were** at school last Friday.*

2 We form the past simple of *be* like this:

singular	plural
I **was**	we **were**
you **were**	you **were**
he/she/it **was**	they **were**

3 We form the negative by adding *not* (*was not, were not*). In speaking and informal writing, we almost always use the short forms *wasn't* and *weren't*.

   *I **wasn't** at home last night.*
   *She **wasn't** at the party.*
   *You **weren't** very happy yesterday.*
   *They **weren't** with us at the concert.*

4 The past simple of *there is(n't) / there are(n't)* is *there was(n't) / there were(n't)*.

   ***There was** a lot of rain yesterday.*
   ***There weren't** any interesting programmes on TV last night.*

Past simple: Was he …? / Were you …?

We form questions by putting the verb before the subject.

***Were** you late on Monday morning?*
***Was** she at the cinema with you?*

Past simple: regular verbs

1 We use the past simple to talk about actions and events in the past.

   *I **played** video games yesterday.*
   *They **liked** the film on Friday.*

2 With regular verbs, we form the past simple by adding *-ed*. It is the same for all subjects.

   *He **closed** the window.*
   *The film **finished** after midnight.*
   *You **phoned** me three times last night.*
   *We **wanted** to see them.*

3 When the verb ends in *-e*, we only add *-d*. When the verb ends in consonant + *-y*, we change the *y* to *i* and then we add *-ed*.

   *We **loved** the concert on Sunday.*
   *They **studied** for a long time before the test.*

UNIT 11
Past simple: irregular verbs

1   **Many English verbs are irregular. This means that the past simple forms are different – they don't have the usual *-ed* ending, for example:**

*go – **went***
*make – **made***
*give – **gave***
*take – **took***
*put – **put***

2   **For every irregular verb, you need to remember the past simple form. There is a list of irregular verbs on page 128.**

Past simple (negative)

We form negatives in the past simple with *didn't* (*did not*) and the base form of the verb. It's the same for both regular and irregular verbs. It's the same for all subjects.

talk	I **didn't talk**.
like	You **didn't like** it.
give	She **didn't give** me a present.
go	He **didn't go** to town.
take	We **didn't take** any photographs.
make	They **didn't make** any money.

Past simple (questions)

We form questions in the past simple with *Did* + subject + the base form of the verb. It's the same for all verbs (regular and irregular) and for all subjects.

see	**Did** I **see** you in town on Saturday?
do	**Did** you **do** the homework last night?
go	**Did** your brother **go** to the same school?
take	**Did** they **take** you to the theatre?

could / couldn't (ability)

To talk about ability in the past, we use *could/ couldn't* + the base form of a verb.

*When I was small, I **could walk** on my hands.*
*We went to London but we **couldn't go** on the London Eye because it was closed.*

UNIT 12
Comparative adjectives

1   **We use the comparative form of the adjective + *than* to compare two things.**

*My sister is **younger than** me.*
*Australia is **smaller than** Brazil.*
*My new smartphone is **better than** the old one.*

2   **With short adjectives, we normally add *-er*.**

*new – new**er***
*quiet – quiet**er***

With adjectives that end in *-e*, we just add *-r*.

*nice – nice**r***
*fine – fine**r***

With adjectives of two syllables that end with consonant + *-y*, we change the *y* to *i* and add *-er*.

*easy – eas**ier***
*healthy – health**ier***

With adjectives that end in consonant + vowel + consonant, we double the final consonant and add *-er*.

*big – bi**gger***
*hot – ho**tter***

3   **With longer adjectives (i.e. with two or more syllables), we don't change the adjective – we put *more* in front of it.**

*expensive – **more expensive***
*dangerous – **more dangerous***

4   **Some adjectives are irregular – this means they have a different comparative form.**

*good – **better***
*bad – **worse***
*far – **further***

one / ones

1   **Sometimes we don't want to repeat a noun. We can use *one* or *ones* in order not to repeat it.**

*The pizza was delicious – I want another (~~pizza~~) **one**.*
*These shoes are very expensive – I want cheaper (~~shoes~~) **ones**.*

2   **We use *one* to replace a singular noun, and *ones* to replace a plural noun.**

*This red shirt is OK, but the blue **one** is nicer. (one replaces shirt)*
*I don't want to play these old games – let's buy some new **ones**. (ones replaces games)*

IRREGULAR VERBS

Base form	Past simple
be	was/were
begin	began
buy	bought
can	could
catch	caught
choose	chose
come	came
do	did
draw	drew
drink	drank
drive	drove
eat	ate
fall	fell
feel	felt
find	found
fly	flew
get	got
give	gave
go	went
have	had
hear	heard
keep	kept
know	knew
learn	learnt/learned
leave	left

Base form	Past simple
light	lit
make	made
meet	met
pay	paid
put	put
read /riːd/	read /red/
ride	rode
run	ran
say	said
see	saw
send	sent
sing	sang
sit	sat
sleep	slept
speak	spoke
stand	stood
take	took
teach	taught
tell	told
think	thought
understand	understood
wake	woke
wear	wore
write	wrote